SEARCH FOR JUSTICE

SEARCH FOR JUSTICE

A Woman's Path to

Renewed Self-Esteem from

the Fear, Shame, and Anger

of Sexual Harassment and

Employment Discrimination

B.J. HOLCOMBE AND
CHARMAINE WELLINGTON

STILLPOINT PUBLISHING
Walpole, NH

STILLP‹   ›ISHING
Building a society that honors The Earth,
Humanity, and The Sacred in All Life.

For a free catalog or ordering information, write
Stillpoint Publishing, Box 640, Walpole, NH 03608, USA
or call
1-800-847-4014 TOLL-FREE (Continental US, except NH)
1-603-756-9281 (Foreign and NH)

This book is manufactured in the United States of America.
Text design by Karen Savary

Published by Stillpoint Publishing, Box 640,
Meetinghouse Road, Walpole, NH 03608

Library of Congress Catalog Card Number: 92-61573

Holcombe, B.J., and Wellington, Charmaine
Search for Justice

ISBN 0-913299-86-3

This book is printed on acid-free, recycled paper to save trees and to
preserve Earth's ecology.

1 3 5 7 9 8 6 4 2

Dedication

To the women—blue-collar and white-collar—who persisted in their search for justice until laws and regulations barring sexual harassment of and employment discrimination against women were in place.

Contents

CONTENTS

Author's Preface:
Charmaine Wellington

Sexual harassment and employment discrimination are a social injustice that blights the lives of talented, dedicated women. They frustrate achievement, thwart purpose and undermine morale of bright, ambitious individuals willing to offer their talents to society. So this social injustice, like a disease, saps the vitality from our society.

And the injustice can infect the whole structure of an organization without being recognized for the epidemic it is—except for those who have been afflicted with the disease. Those women whose opportunities and potential are being blocked by the social injustice of employment discrimination and sexual harassment know the symptoms: fear, shame and anger. And they're ready for the injustice to be diagnosed and remedied.

Yet sexual harassment and employment discrimination are a secret epidemic—ignored, misdiagnosed as a woman's personal problem, and allowed to proliferate—unless one is in the position to recognize how widespread the problem is.

Within a few weeks of being elected president of my local chapter of the National Organization for Women, I discovered that I would regularly be getting calls from troubled, angry women desperately searching for help. B.J. was one of those callers. She was in the final stage of her search for justice from Shell Oil Company, a search that had just been frustrated by the out-of-court settlement of her lawsuit.

As she told me of the sexual harassment and discrimination she had weathered as the first woman oil production worker at Shell Oil Company's East Bay, a barrier island off Louisiana's Mississippi delta, I was struck by how familiar her experiences sounded.

Like B.J., I had been for the past five years waging my own search for justice. As the only woman professor in an all-male university department, I had been up against the same male resistance to women in the workplace that B.J. had endured. My university colleagues' manners were better than B.J.'s colleagues'—university professors prefer verbal assassinations and inner-office manipulations to rape attempts—but the spirit in both her workplace and mine was the same. Some of our colleagues clearly felt a not-so-suppressed anger that women should aspire to the same wages and social status as men and were unwilling to accept women as equals, as individuals, and as colleagues. That anger leaked out in both overt and covert abuse of our autonomy, achievements, and dreams. And the institutions we worked for condoned the abuse through inattention or rationalization.

Listening to B.J. brought home the truth for me once again: blue collar or white, women are all potential or actual hostages of that agenda of prejudice and discrimination that I call gender terrorism.

Yet B.J. and I both believe that the truth can set you free, so we joined up to tell the truth of what she lived through. We hope that by telling the whole truth of sexual harassment and discrimination at East Bay, we can shine a brighter light on that often obscured and denied face of injustice against women. And we hope that B.J.'s story of endurance and resistance will inspire more women—and men—to join in a search for justice for women in the workplace.

Author's Preface:
B.J. Holcombe

᪥

Search for Justice makes my life an open book. I was reared in a family of eight children. Each of us firmly believed we could be anything we chose to be, because we were often told this as children.

We were really close as a family. By today's standards, we were not ideal, but we all felt loved by parents and siblings. I learned hard work at an early age. A lot of desires for material possessions were unmet, although basic needs for living and survival were taught.

My mother, Nora—my father called her Jim—would often read the Bible to us around the kitchen table. I was much closer to my father, but I had a lot of respect for my mother's religious beliefs and teachings.

I attended Sunday school every Sunday and even taught a Sunday School class when I was in high school.

We all have the power within us to make things happen. We need to be thoughtful enough to never abuse this power.

It is the God part of us: our conscience should be our guide. The largest obstacles can be the best learning experiences. Even though the mountain may appear too high to climb, you can only do one step at a time, and if you persevere you will reach the top.

My presence at an offshore oil facility, surrounded by male workers, by itself created change. I loved the work I was doing and made many friends and won their respect. However, I didn't feel that I owed my loyalty to a company that would not protect my rights as a human being; I refused to cross over the line to defend them against someone else that they had treated so unjustly. I felt I was giving up everything at a great loss in order to follow my conscience.

I had succeeded on the job one step at a time, but I was knocked off the mountain before I reached the top for the view. Then to have the patience and strength for one step at a time into another unknown world, the world of justice, seemed almost impossible. That is the mountain I still climb.

Until the company will promote women from within the system, and treat them justly, I will take one step at a time. I hope this can be a team effort. With the help of others, we will teach human rights and justice for all, without the anger, hurt, and deprivation that is so commonplace now.

My hope is that this book will help others to feel less alone when confronted with similar circumstances and that it will perhaps teach others that to create this harassment is a violation of human rights.

Note: I have changed some of the names of the people mention in this account.

Acknowledgements

❧

From both authors, many thanks to Meredith Young-Sowers and Dorothy Seymour of Stillpoint Publishing for their support, patience, and creativity, especially in the final stages of development of *Search for Justice*. And thank you to Don Boose of the University of West Florida Technical-Vocational Computer Laboratory for his technical assistance.

B.J. Holcombe acknowledges the encouragement of her husband, Joe Holcombe, in inspiring her to begin writing about her experiences, and her father, Charles Poynter, for instilling in her the determination to do what she knows is right.

Charmaine Wellington is grateful for the ongoing support of her family: Rita and Jim Williams, Peggy Wattling, and Bill Wattling, Jr. She also thanks Jackie Johnson Maughan and Susan X. Day for their insightful, attentive reading of the manuscript and their helpful advice.

Both authors recognize with gratitude the important role the other played in shaping this stage of their search for justice.

I
EQUALITY

❦

When we Americans who are women take jobs, we expect to have the opportunity to succeed according to our effort and potential. We expect to be able to work without suffering discrimination on account of our gender. But we often find this expectation dashed. Equality, a fundamental ideal of American government and society, is in fact not yet won by women in the workplace.

Every day the six o'clock news tells the story: a woman's employer or fellow worker has sexually harassed her, or denied her promotions or work opportunities. To them, just because she's a woman, she's fair game.

We all know what sexual harassment and discrimination feel like: indignation, fear, and shame rise up within us like a sickness. Sexual harassment and discrimination in the workplace can feel like being caught in a trap, because while we could brush off unwanted advances from a stranger at a party, we might hesitate to brush off or talk back to a boss for fear of losing a needed job.

Sexual harassment and discrimination are unjust violations of women's right to equal treatment, and women want justice.

1

GENDER TERRORISM

❦

B.J. Holcombe was the first woman oil production worker on Shell Oil Company's "men-only" island called East Bay, situated off the Mississippi River delta. The country was rugged, and so were the men she worked with.

Her story is one of survival and transcendence. Her painful struggle, her brave determination, and her resourceful responses show us that we can all survive and become stronger, more self-affirming women by accepting the social injustice of sexual harassment and discrimination as a personal challenge.

❧ Before I became the first female offshore oil production worker at Shell Oil's East Bay, I'd always felt scorn for wives who were abused or female employees who were harassed by oversexed bosses. "Why were these women so weak, so vulnerable?" I'd wonder. "They're the cause of their own problems. They should just leave." I'd congratulate myself on my belief that I would never put up with such disrespect. I'd never been physically or emotionally intimidated by anyone, even when up against the roughest, most ignorant types.

Now, as my eyes locked in a stare-down contest with Beth Hess, Employee Relations Assistant for Shell Oil company, I remembered my arrogant attitude as I mentally reviewed the last eight years, during which I myself endured ugly, humiliating sexual harassment.

I remembered incident after incident. My male co-workers tried to use sexual intimidation and insult to force me out of a well-paying job that I loved. I remembered the night a man almost raped me, another man who repeatedly masturbated in front of me, the one who urinated on me, and the other sexual displays and harassment I endured. I remembered the reports about these incidents sent to supervisors who ignored them. I remembered my long, slow rise through the ranks, a much slower rise than my good work deserved.

Now, staring into Beth Hess's eyes, I sat in a small bedroom in the living quarters of the East Bay facility, Shell's main oil production site on a barrier island at the mouth of the Mississippi River in southern Lousiana. In the delta heat of August 21, 1988, the tension was palpable.

The foreman had called me back from the oil platforms in the surrounding marshy areas to talk with Beth Hess, who came the ninety miles from One Shell Square in New Orleans to talk with me face to face. She and Production Foreman John Town, head of the entire operation at East Bay, sat across from me in easy chairs while I uncomfortably arranged my six feet, one inch of height onto the small straight chair. We sat in a supervisor's spartan room, decorated only by the ominous blank eye of his TV set, the room Hess was using for her investigation of charges of gender-based discrimination and sexual harassment brought by my co-worker, Jenny Black.

Beth Hess's painted nails, thin blue eyeliner, slim build, and blond hair gave her a delicate look somewhat at odds with the steel-toed work boots and jeans she had donned to come onto the work location. Gazing at her, I recalled our last interview three years before, when I and several other female workers tried to tell her what had been happening to us at East Bay. Today, her usually outgoing manner was subdued, but three years earlier her face had looked even less self-assured.

At that time, just as she was today, she was visiting East Bay to investigate problems in employees' work relationships. Two other female workers and I had cornered her at the end of a catwalk by the females' quarters, demanding that she listen to our stories of horror. But Beth had slipped out from between us, saying that she needed to make a phone call. She had never come back, and the next day she took the helicopter to her posh offices, leaving us frustrated and astonished at her indifference to our situation as female workers. Sexual harassment had continued unchecked after her last visit, so this time I expected nothing but trouble.

Leaning back in her chair with her fingers comfortably twined together, Beth began explaining the reason for her visit: Jenny Ann Black had asked her attorney to file a complaint of sexual harassment against Shell Oil. For six years, Jenny had been a co-worker of mine, but this week she hadn't shown up for work. I'd been wondering where she was.

"Have you read any of the affidavits Jenny filed?"

The question surprised me. "No," I said. "I knew nothing of her intentions." I knew that Jenny's problems with her supervisor had recently come to a climax but hadn't expected the naive twenty-five-year-old to take matters into her own hands.

Beth's eyes narrowed skeptically as she opened the attache sitting beside her chair. She handed me a statement, cleanly typed and signed by Jenny herself. "Here. Read this and tell us what you know about her allegations."

John Town spoke up for the first time. He was dressed in the slacks and sport shirt that announced to everyone, "I'm Shell Oil Management." He said to me, "You owe your loyalty to the company, B.J. Remember."

"I don't owe nothing to nobody!" I snapped back. Threats always raised my hackles, especially threats by an employer using my job to control me. To my mind, I have always offered fair work in return for a fair salary, and I owe nothing but the truth.

Beth diverted our argument. "I don't see how Jenny's allegations can be true. They're impossible."

This, too, touched a nerve in me, for in some ways Jenny's experience had been harder than mine. Jenny was just nineteen when she was hired to work offshore along with me. A protected New Orleans Catholic away from home for the first time, Jenny was also a virgin. Yet her supervisor's best friend had begun a sexual relationship with her about the time there was talk of firing her, promising her that he would protect her job. Jenny was too young and foolish take my advice and refuse his attentions.

I skimmed Jenny's statement, tingling with uneasiness. Each incident Jenny listed was familiar to me. I'd either witnessed them myself or observed their immediate consequences. As I read, my resolution formed. Because I loved the truth, I would not testify against Jenny Black when she had her day in court.

I looked up to meet what seemed to be a sly look on Beth's face. That look provoked my ire.

"What kind of a person are you that you can try to use me against Jenny? You know that everything she's alleging here is the absolute truth. We tried to tell you three years ago about the situation here."

Beth's eyes dropped, but she echoed John's warning of a moment before. "Just remember, you need to represent the company's best interests."

Eight years of swallowed anger burst out in a moment of decision. "I don't owe this company shit! I've worked for every dime they've paid me. Have you ever been pissed on? I have— at East Bay. Have you ever been raped? I almost was—at East Bay. I don't owe Shell Oil nothing." I was tight-jawed with rage.

"I don't believe this," Beth countered, jerking to the edge of her chair.

"Well, you'd better, because I'm not going to lie to protect Shell Oil."

John piped in, "Employee Relations will work it out, B.J. Tell her all of it right now." As production foreman, John had expected employees to file complaints through company channels. To his mind, Jenny broke the rules by consulting a lawyer, and he was angry. He didn't seem to know or care that supervisors dismissed our reports, blocked the proper channels for redress of complaints, intimidated us, distorted evaluations of our work performance and even threated to fire us when we reported harassment and discrimination. In fact, some of those supervisors were harassers themselves!

"If I do tell it all, John, it will hurt a lot of people, including you."

We all paused and reflected on the possibilities. I was in a cat-and-mouse game, and I was the mouse.

"Before I start talking," I said to Beth, "I want to talk with John outside."

She nodded, and we lurched stiffly to our feet and walked to the catwalk at the end of the long hall.

The intense humidity and heat of August in the Mississippi delta hit us as we stepped through the door onto the metal grating. We both reached for cigarettes, tossing our spent matches into the split dried mud over which the buildings at East Bay perched. We looked anxiously into each other's eyes.

I felt that I understood John Town. A middle-aged man of Italian descent, his black hair was greying, his middle was thickening, and his large brown eyes looked distorted by the lenses of reading glasses. He must have had ulcers, for he ordered Maalox by the case and kept a bottle on his desk. In short, John had given his life to Shell Oil. He couldn't let himself question the company.

I started talking first. "You know, John, that if I tell this woman everything, it will cost jobs, maybe even marriages. You know you're not innocent yourself." If I blew the whistle on the gender terrorists at East Bay, the shock waves would unsettle the lives of innocent wives and children. I knew I wouldn't lie to save Shell Oil from Jenny Black, but ought I also tell the truth?

"Let's get it out, B.J. At least, tell her what you know."

"Okay," I said, taking a deep breath to fend off the nausea that swept over me. The moment of decision, which had been looming ahead of me for eight and a half years, had come. "Let's get it over with." The slow arc of my flying cigarette seemed to last forever. I turned and passed through the dark doorway.

Inside once again, I told Beth Hess everything for the record that I and the three other women on my crew had been trying to tell Shell Oil for years.

Eight years and nine months before, without even giving me a lock on my bedroom door, Shell Oil sent me onto an offshore facility where I would be the only woman among about 175 men. Without planning for the inevitable complications of introducing a woman into a workplace, they put me in the midst of men who felt they were defending the last male-only workplace in America. They persistently ignored our reports of threats, intimidation, and manipulation, ignored our achievements, blocked our opportunities. Shell Oil had set me up—set all of us up—to bear the brunt of ugly discrimination. I stayed with my job because I wouldn't back down, wouldn't give in, wouldn't let the bigots drive me away from the Bay. I had stayed because I was stronger than they were. But I was also angry, and it was time to tell Beth Hess why.

Hess fired at me the questions that Jenny's charges had raised. I gave her all the details about the night I escaped from the rapist who invaded my room while I slept, amazed that I had to repeat what I had already reported to the company immediately after the incident. Even though the rape attempt was his second attack on me, the company had been reluctant to fire the man. The company had also failed to fire people for fighting on company property, for drinking on the job, and for a number of offenses that were supposed to be a basis for dismissal.

Beth then asked me if I knew about Jenny Black's affair with Dex Pace. "Certainly," I said. "Everyone at East Bay knew about it. I did accidentally walk into Jenny's room while they were having sex once, though, so I had first-hand knowledge." Hess's questions went on and on, and I had first-hand evidence in answer to most of them. I knew how slipshod and capricious Shell Oil's Employee Relations office was, and if Jenny's lawyer wanted to call me to the witness stand I would tell it all. And not only women had been harassed, but blacks and younger men as well. One of my co-workers had threated a young male college student who had just been hired. The angry Shell hand had promised to "bend him over like a shot gun and rape him."

As I spilled the accumulated stories, naming names, facts, and dates, I thought about the journals and tapes I'd been keeping the entire time. No lawyer would catch me unable to recall a detail, because from the first incident I had written down everything that happened. I would be a formidable witness.

I also knew that by telling Beth Hess everything, I was putting my life in jeopardy. The men who harassed me for years would escalate their actions now that I was telling the law about them. I would not be safe at East Bay, maybe not even in my own home near Pensacola, Florida, for the men's revenge would be intense. I would have to leave, and that meant giving up a career, nine years' advancement toward retirement, and challenging work that I loved.

That evening as I stuffed my duffle bag with clothes, boxed up my TV set, and took my posters down from the walls of my dim room, I cried. The moral outrage that had buoyed me up through the long interview had evaporated, leaving a residue of regrets. This had been my home for every other week for more than eight years. Had I failed, finally, in my determination to last at East Bay? Had I failed the women who were working here and at other offshore oil facilities? I felt lost and alone, as if something precious had suddenly been taken from me.

What was it that I had lost? Certainly, my job, but something more, I thought, as I rustled through the drawers under my bunk. I found a long-forgotten pouch of chewing tobacco, the tobacco inside dried and brittle. I hadn't chewed for years, but the sight of it stirred memories.

At least six years before, while I had been replacing a metal grating stair tread on one of the platforms, Sly, another member of my work gang, stopped to say a few words. Automatically, he held his pouch out to me, proffering a dare at the same time: "Oh, you don't chew tobacco because you're a woman, right?"

"Sure I do," I said, and took a wad for myself. I took it, not because I was curious, not because I wanted to feel powerful, but to show him that tobacco didn't make him a man. A woman could do just what he was doing—chewing tobacco and working on an oil platform.

That first chew of tobacco was very sweet, but it burned my mouth. I kept it up, though, for the next two years, buying my own and offering it to others as my male co-workers did, all in the effort to fit in. I'd been trying to win acceptance.

But now as I was packing, with teardrops spotting the dust in the now-empty drawer, the memory of those adaptations and concessions embittered me. I had become a woman who chewed tobacco, swore along with the most vigorous of the work gang, and pushed her way to the top of a pecking order through force of personality. Although I'd been a vegetarian for five years before coming to East Bay, I even changed my eating habits. I was weeping over the loss of a past self: the patient, moderate woman who had nursed the sick and the aged.

Besides moral outrage, then, was grief over lost innocence. And guilt.

Had I aped male behavior too much in a futile effort to win men's approval? Although I'd given up chewing tobacco within just a few months, I still walked out of the barge cabin that day years ago when Lightning had called my friend Lloyd a "nigger" behind his back. I, whom Lightning called a "cunt" and a "pussy," had felt powerless to change such a man. Had I become a part of their bigotry by turning my back on it?

As a girl growing up in the coal-mining country of Kentucky, I worked alongside my five brothers to trap and hunt and fell trees, seeing nothing inappropriate to my sex in these activities. So from the first day at East Bay, I had that toughness in me. I could defend myself and be authoritative—willing to "kick ass," as the phrase goes. When in the first week Dick Samuels the welder refused to work with me, a trained welder myself, I "one-upped" him in the masculine style. I made him feel his age by pointing out that I might be starting out at the bottom but I was going to be around a lot longer than he.

I'd been scared, but, just like men, I wouldn't let them see it, I thought guiltily.

Swept by these currents of emotion, I envisioned the bitter, woman-hating face of Dick Samuels, and suddenly an idea came like a lighthouse to guide me through the swirling waters. I, a woman, had a right to be there. Justice demanded that I, as well as others, be treated fairly, not harassed, intimidated, made to conform to manners irrelevant to the job. No matter the concessions, adaptations, and evasions I was guilty of, my standards of justice remained untainted, and I would stand up for the truth.

With a sigh that seemed to rise from my very soul, I sat down to write, as I so often had before. I wrote my letter of resignation, and then I remembered the dildo that had been anonymously put in my lunch bag just months before. When I reported the incident, I left it in the safekeeping of the night clerk. I would have to go get it. But my eyes were swollen from crying, and I never let anyone at East Bay see me cry.

The cool water from the bathroom sink and the night air helped my eyes feel more natural, but Norman, the night clerk, noticed anyway. "You been crying, B.J.? What's going on?" I knew he was curious. Everyone at East Bay knew by now that I spent the afternoon with an Employee Relations representative. But Norman was talking with Dan Underwood, whom I believed to be responsible for the dildo.

"Just problems, Norm." I felt a pang at not confiding in him. We'd always been friends. But now I would have to go alone. "You still keeping that dildo?" I asked, without looking at Dan.

"You bet."

"Can I have it? It may come in handy soon."

The next morning I handed Operations Foreman Roy Barker my resignation. He was aghast. "You can't do this, B.J. You've been here too long. Whatever the problems are, we'll work them out." But I knew that wasn't true. I and the other women had tried to no avail to get the company to protect us. Jenny was right; the only recourse left was the Law.

13

"It can't be helped," I cried. "I should have done this a long time ago."

When the boat arrived that took employees back and forth between the barrier island and the terminal south of New Orleans, I carried my bags on board and then sadly stood on deck. I watched the graceful landing of the seaplane that carried mail. It would take my letter of resignation back to One Shell Square, and I would begin my long legal battle against Shell Oil and my slow recovery from the gender terrorism I'd endured. As the launch pulled away from the dock into the marsh-lined canal, I didn't look back.

I hired on with Shell Oil almost by accident. Joe, my husband, had given me the idea. Disenchanted with his job as a civilian machine tool technologist for the Navy, he had been bringing home applications forms, some from major oil companies in the South. One day when I was doing housework and muttering to myself over the small paycheck I was earning as a nurse in a convalescent center in Florida, I found the applications in a kitchen drawer. On an impulse, I filled them out and put them in the mail before Joe got home. After all, I was worth more than that convalescent center was paying me.

Weeks went by without my even thinking about those applications again, but somehow within myself I was preparing for a change. Nursing at the Cliffs Extended Care Facility was not the career I was hoping for. As a paramedic in the Air Force I'd been dropped by helicopter into disaster areas to administer first aid assistance to victims of air liner crashes.

I'd even operated my own clinic. The gleaming hallways and hushed tempo of the Cliffs made me feel closed in. My life lacked adventure, challenge—and decent wages.

When I got the call from One Shell Square asking me to drive the 200 miles from Pensacola to New Orleans for tests and an interview, I turned to Joe, feeling a surge of excitement, and said, "This is something I want to do."

We began to build castles in the air. I would make eight dollars an hour, three more than I was making at the time. The high salary would fuel our hopes of early retirement. We'd survived the lean times together while we earned our degrees, and now, with just moderate income from our two jobs, we wanted more. We could build a new home, buy a boat for skin diving in the Gulf of Mexico, and live a more active life. Furthermore, I never liked having to rely so heavily on my husband for our mutual support. I was used to paying my own way, and once again I would enjoy the satisfaction of contributing hefty sums to our household. And I would have every other week off.

We evaluated the drawbacks seriously, too. When the job took me into the oil fields for seven days every other week, we would have to be separated. Still, Joe and I had been separated in the Air Force, where separations came with the job. Neither one of us particularly liked being without the other's company, but we respected the other person's need to grow. We knew from experience that being away from one another for a while always made being together more meaningful. After a long evening of excited talk, we looked one another in the eyes, and Joe told me, "Go for it!"

I arrived early at One Shell Square for the initial battery of tests and a physical examination in early November of 1979. Although the morning air was crisp and cool, and the bright sky promised a beautiful day to come. I was too busy to notice the weather. The fifty-five-story building that houses the American offices of Dutch-owned Shell Oil Company, the world's second richest oil company, wasn't hard to find. The tallest in that city built on oystershell-filled swamp, its stark white exterior gleamed against against the vivid blue New Orleans sky. I felt awed by the scope of the vast multinational company, the role it played in powering the world's economy. It employs people in oil production, refinement, distribution, and sales. The company pumps oil from locations all over the world, including the coasts of South Africa, Cameroon, Brazil, and, of course, the United States. I was hoping to work on Shell's East Bay, the oil production site off of the Mississippi River delta. I felt puny, for all of my six foot, one inch of height. Little did I know that eight and a half years later, Employee Relations Supervisors whose offices were at such a dizzying height would be begging me not to sue Shell.

I pushed through the revolving doors and felt another pang of awe at the size of that enormous lobby. The security guard's directions to the testing area were easy to follow. When I got there, I saw that I was just one of about fifty people hoping for the same opportunity. I spent the next five hours taking Shell's exams to determine my reading skill, my math skill, my mechanical aptitudes, and so on. The tests were like many high school aptitude tests: multiple choice with computer-graded sheets. Afterwards, I was asked to wait while my results were tabulated. Within just twenty minutes I was called into the personnel office, congratulated on my high score, and asked a series of questions about my application. "Does your husband know what you're doing?" the personnel officer inquired.

After my medical examination two weeks later I was asked back for interviews at least five times. To the first one, I brought Joe along. Since Personnel seemed concerned about my husband's attitude, I thought he should reassure them of his support face-to-face. My last interview, scheduled the day before I was to report to East Bay, was with the superintendent of the Coastal Offshore East division, Ervin Floyd, who had been on vacation during the six weeks' interview process.

On January 2, 1980, I ascended by elevator to the fifty-second story of One Shell Square and walked to Ervin Floyd's office. I entered into the elegantly furnished office with an equally elegant secretary, thinking wryly of episodes of *Dallas*. She escorted me into Mr. Floyd's office immediately. I was startled by the tension I felt there. Although this short, balding, square-faced man rose from his black leather chair and extended a hand, there was no warmth at all in his drawled greeting. As I sat down, the array of ornately-framed photographs of offshore oil platforms and drilling rigs reflected off his thick black-framed glasses.

He came directly to the point. In clipped sentences crackling with resentment, he told me that I should never have been hired. He told me that women were not wanted at East Bay.

"I will personally do whatever is necessary to get rid of you," he hissed with the venom of a good-ole'-boy betrayed.

Everything necessary had been said, he made clear. The interview was over. But he had not reckoned on my determination to take this job and keep it. I walked to the door, shaken inwardly but determined not to let him stand in my way. Shell had hired me, and one man was not going to keep me away. Hand on the half-opened door, I turned around and leveled my own firm and final statement: "Mr. Floyd, I will make you the best employee you have ever had at East Bay." I walked out, leaving the door open behind me.

The next time I met Ervin Floyd, I was covered with sweat and hardened by six months' challenging labor at Shell's East Bay. Although he had made daily phone calls to East Bay's Production Foreman, Hoss Blackman, Floyd had not been able to drum me out yet. As if to tell me he was not yet through with me, he offered me a chew of tobacco from his pouch.

When B.J. asserted her claim to a job with Shell Oil in 1980, the Equal Employment Opportunity Commission had just formally defined sexual harassment and discrimination. Written regulations against hiring discrimination had also recently been put in place.

But B.J.'s experience proves there can be a wide gap between having a legal right to a job and being accepted as a worker. She had the law behind her, but that was the problem: the law was behind her, and she was leading the way.

Still, she joined the workforce at East Bay, thus claiming her right to equal opportunities for meaningful, well-paid work. She had to struggle against the social resistance of the "old-school" point of view. That view says that men need jobs more than women, that men need higher pay more than women, and that men work harder and better than women at manual work. She accepted the struggle, even though creating change in a whole group's social attitudes is a difficult burden for a person to bear. *Only years later was B.J. able to appraise what the effort cost her.*

Many of the women who have taken on the burden of creating change have recognized that no change comes easily. They have made the choice to weather the resistance, no matter the cost. B.J.'s success at bearing harassment and discrimination for eight years, during which she endured physical threats and other humiliations, testified to her tenacious determination to win her just place. But when the company attempted to manipulate her into perjuring herself, thus subverting the final authority of fairness and justice, she saw that attempt as a violation of a sacred principle. For her, if the courts were not honest, what point the struggle? For B.J., as for many women, a line had been drawn in the sand, a line she had to cross.

For any woman in a situation like B.J.'s, her own values must be the ultimate authority. It is women's right to decide where to draw the line between treatment they will accept and treatment they will challenge.

II
ASPIRATION

A truly equal, just society is one that recognizes the full complexity of every human being, male or female. It offers every human being, regardless of race, creed, sex, or any other social factor, the opportunity to express her potential fully in whatever ways are not harmful to others. Meaningful work, work that allows the full play of one's talents and interests, is one channel through which an individual's potential flows.

Justice to women requires that they have the opportunity to aspire to success in meaningful work, even if the choice of the particular field is unusual for women. Women must, in justice, be permitted the right to undertake, and succeed at, the kind of work that suits them.

2

WALTZING PAST THE "MEN ONLY" SIGN: MY ARRIVAL AT EAST BAY

✥

The desire for better work and better wages are natural to any human being, including B.J. Her drive to enter the field she wanted and to get paid what she felt she deserved grew out of her own self-respect. She also wanted more from her workplace than just a means of supporting herself and her family: she wanted an opportunity to exercise her talents and realize her potential.

B.J.'s hunger for meaningful work, as well as her talents in understanding mechanical and technical systems, led her initially into nursing, a traditionally female occupation. She could, however, apply those same talents to the "non-traditional" work with pipes and wrenches offered at East Bay and earn a far higher salary, better benefits, and more liberal retirement advantages. So why shouldn't she enter that "non-traditional" workplace?

◦✿ The dislike in Ervin Floyd's face haunted me as I settled into my Holiday Inn room on the evening of my last night on shore. I was scheduled to go by boat to East Bay from Venice, Louisiana, seventy-fives miles down the Mississippi from New Orleans. I had to be at the boat terminal by 7:00 A.M. I had been hired, and report to work I would, in spite of Ervin Floyd's threats. I double-checked to make sure that the papers from Personnel showing that I was a bona fide employee were in my attache case. I recalled the photographs of oil rigs on the walls behind and around Floyd. His bulky shape seemed to form a barrier between me and my destination, the work location on the margin between the delta and the Gulf, between me and my dream of better pay and success.

I found myself thinking about my father, lanky and wiry from years of coal mining in Kentucky. He raised his eight children to be as fiercely independent as he was. He made no arbitrary distinctions between his five daughters and his three sons. He didn't have to. We were as individual as he was. He and Momma demanded that we do well in school, be truthful, work hard, and expect fair treatment. "You can be anything you want to be, B.J.," Daddy used to tell me as I helped him build the smokehouse behind our country home.

"Could I?" I thought to myself, remembering the set of Ervin Floyd's face as I set my alarm clock for 4:30 A.M. and prepared to make my goodnight call to Joe back at home. I suspected that it wasn't going to be easy.

Shell Oil had hired me because I was exceptionally quali-

24

fied. I had walked into their offices with a college degree and a nursing diploma, two years' work experience as a welder at General Motors in Michigan and as a temporary telephone installer, and two years' experience as a paramedic in the Air Force. I earned high praise from every supervisor in demanding blue collar jobs, and I had skills with tools and procedures that are used in off-shore oil production. My scores on their tests were very high. Furthermore, I never was really delicate. Having been six feet, one inch tall since eighth grade, I never doubted my capacity to accomplish a physically demanding feat. I had the physical hardiness required by manual labor. How could they not hire me? To refuse would have made them liable to sex discrimination charges, although the thought hadn't really occurred to me at the time. In fact, if they'd refused to hire me, I would never have questioned them; most likely, I'd have walked away wondering where I'd gone wrong.

Shell Oil would get the best employee they ever had, I told myself firmly as I threw the sheets over me and turned out the light. That determination and self-esteem would help me face down intolerance and injustice during the next eight years. Not knowing what lay ahead of me, I was at that very moment accepting the burden of creating change when I promised myself to make Ervin Floyd change his mind about me. Later, that fighting spirit, the inheritance of my family life, would be supported by another, and unexpected, motivation: love of the work itself. But at the time I knew only that I could prove my worth, and that I would.

Sleep eluded me that night as I tried to imagine what the next day would bring. When the alarm clock jangled me out of my light sleep, I was into my blue jeans, sweatshirt, and steel-toed work boots in five minutes. As I took a last look around the room to make sure that I had left nothing behind, I dismissed without regret the nursing position I'd resigned. Now it was time for me to reach for a new future, new challenges, new wages. I was an oil production worker. No looking back.

To reach the boat terminal for East Bay facilities, I had to drive seventy-five miles south out of New Orleans on Louisiana Highway 23 to the small fishing community of Venice, long an outlet for several oil companies' employees and their supplies. I rolled down the windows to the chilly morning air, nervously smoking cigarettes and sipping black McDonald's coffee from my thermos filled the night before. This was an adventure, and I was going to experience it as fully as I could.

The landscape's uniqueness, too strange to be called beauty, beguiled me as I drove. An exotic rosy dawn broke as I neared stinky Port Sulphur illuminating the shrimp boats and barges in the canals and bayous, the veins of the Mississippi delta system. The delta is no-nonsense country; nothing is decorated. Every building and facility is devoted to work of some kind, and paint, if used at all, is used to prolong the life of the wood, not to please the eye. The town's shabby straightforwardness appealed to me. I drove on. Further south of Port Sulphur the road got more bumpy, but the traffic, which had been light, got more active. Twenty-five jolting miles later Venice's fish processing and fertilizer plant announced that I had come to the end of the road and was about to step off into the unknown.

I was right on time: 6:45 A.M. The large yellow scallop shell proclaimed that this was Shell property. It sat atop a sea-green warehouse behind a six-foot mesh wire fence. The terrain was flat and grassy; the road was a crushed oyster-shell surface that crunched as my tires rolled slowly through the entrance into what was obviously the employees' parking lot. Beat-up pickups splattered with red mud alternated with massive, dated Cadillacs. Men of various sizes purposefully pulled duffles from trunks and strode towards the docks of the marshy canal. Obviously, I would follow them.

I drew my Dodge Colt alongside another car that had just pulled in, dumped the cold coffee out of my car window, and shut the car up tight. I would be gone for a week; there was sure to be rain in this stormy southern climate. As I was lifting my old Air Force duffle from my trunk, a tall red-haired man stepped up. He was wearing western-style boots with pointed toes, comfortably worn blue jeans, and a blue shirt with imitation mother-of-pearl buttons at the chest pocket flaps. I was intrigued by the touch of the dandy about him.

"You must be the new woman we've been hearing about. Here, let me carry that for you." His voice was slow as cane syrup pouring over corn grits.

"No, thanks. I'll carry it," I said, mentally noting the chivalrous offer as I picked up my own duffle. They had heard about me, had they? Was my being hired a subject of discussion? Why? But I brushed my questions aside and stuck out my hand to shake his.

"I'm Barbara. Glad to meet you. Can you tell me how to find the Thunderboy?" That was the name of the launch that was supposed to carry me the sixteen miles to the offshore barrier island called East Bay.

"I'm Harley, but folks call me Padre. If you're going to East Bay, we'll all be going out on the same boat. The Thunderboy leaves at seven, Thundergirl at eight."

Padre and I walked toward the dock across the oyster-shell

parking lot, which gleamed blindingly in the morning sun. A sixty-five-foot passenger speedboat was floating there, a long, low boat with a blue strip against the white side just above the water line. The front two-thirds was a series of windows with curtains drawn. As we stepped inside I saw a long center aisle with padded seats like pews on either side. A group playing cards occupied a table at the bow. There must have been room for more than fifty people. I had never been on such a large boat before, and I felt a bit like a kid that my mother had taken to visit a stranger. Although only ten or twelve men were seated here and there, all eyes turned on me and stuck. I was more than just the new kid on the block.

I quickly moved halfway up the aisle and slid onto one of the long benches, scooting up against the window where I could peek out at the country and at the same time survey the faces of my new work partners. I hadn't anticipated causing such a reaction. To me, Shell Oil was a high-paying job that would bring new challenges, but evidently, to these men I was something different, foreign, an alien. I couldn't read their scrutinizing looks to tell whether they were hostile or just curious, but uneasiness tingled through me.

I pulled the curtain back and turned my attention toward the view. I'd chosen the side opposite the dock, so I could see the marshy margins of the other bank. It was typical Gulf Coast saltmarsh: olive green clumps of grasses growing two feet out of shallow water. A small egret waded with majestic deliberation, occasionally darting its long neck at some water creature too small for me to see from my seat in the boat. Once it came up with a small fish grasped horizontally in its narrow beak. With a deft upward jerk of its head, it tossed the fish into the air, lending it a quarter twist, and took it head first into its throat. I loved this peaceful landscape.

Turning back to the men who were waiting sleepily, smoking cigarettes or snapping cards onto the table, I relaxed a bit for the first time in days.

A young man clumped down the three steps to the seating area and came over to me. He had to pull a paperback out of his back pocket so he could bend at the hip before he slid in.

"I'm Bill," he said, holding out a clean, well-maintained hand. He was about twenty, a bit plump, and wore the kind of glasses in style on college campuses. He was not at all the burly, greasy oil rig worker I had expected.

"I'm Barbara. Glad to know you."

Bill told me about himself as we watched the launch quickly fill up with the remaining passengers. He was going to college on the weeks that alternated with his weekly hitches at East Bay. The college, which specialized in training petroleum engineers, was set up to accommodate people on this industry-wide week on-week off schedule. The schedule was demanding, he said, but the education and travel made up for it.

Getting acquainted with this friendly young man, I felt a surge of optimisim and excitement as the men on the dock dropped the heavy tie-ups onto the boat's bow and stern, and the motor's low warm-up rumble shifted into a higher pitch. We labored into the channel, then lurched forward into an even higher gear. Soon we were travelling at a good clip of about thirty knots. I stared, mesmerized, at the rippling, thick brown water of the mighty, muddy Mississippi and wondered if its color would change as we neared the Gulf. Well out into the river now, I watched the massive freight ships with decks piled high with what looked like train cars. On flagpoles atop cranes that soared above the decks, flags from foreign countries flew—most merchant marine vessels are registered in other countries to avoid United States taxes and regulations—but the Stars and Stripes were always visible as well. Our launch slowed as we neared other work vessels, barges or fishing boats that ran up or down the wide, working river. The trip was supposed to take us sixteen miles, so I expected to have an hour and a half to enjoy my first opportunity to be on the granddad of the American river system.

About forty-five minutes later the launch lurched to the left and headed into a narrower pass fringed with marshland. We were not going to the Gulf at all! The water ran more swiftly, and I could feel the boat straining against it. My own sense of urgency intensified as we passed a structure on the bank with the red, white, and blue badge of Chevron. "That must be an oil well," I thought to myself. It was nothing like the huge rocker-arm assemblies that dotted the landscape of the South. On this there were no moving parts. Years later I would become fascinated by and master the pressure gradient principles and gas lift systems by which these wells flowed. Right now the series of tremendous valves, all black in color, just looked like knobs of a Tinker Toy set stacked one on top of the other. The heads of the bolts that held the valves together were of tremendous size, bigger than my fist. I'd always been physically strong, but I knew by looking at that structure that I would be handling more massive tools than I had ever worked with before. My hands were itching to get at them.

After another fifteen minutes the boat began to slow down. Bill told me that we were nearing the living quarters, or "the quarters," as they were called. At least two dozen of the same sea-green metal buildings as at the terminal sat on fifteen-foot pilings on the treeless mile-long barrier island between the river and the Gulf.

We clambered to our feet as the boat docked, picking up duffle bags and luggage from the deck as we stepped onto the pier. I followed the general movement toward the buildings, walking on the metal grating catwalks that were elevated over the swampy soil, until someone pointed out the office and told me to report to Lewis Pastee in there.

Pulling open the green metal door onto a long hallway, I asked the man about to emerge where I might find Mr. Pastee.

"You don't need to see Lew. He works for me. I'm Hoss," he said, holding out a work-toughened hand. I could predict the firmness of the grip before I even grasped it.

My self-consciousness that I was a woman among men resurfaced uncomfortably at his macho tone. Although I was a bit taller than Hoss, I got the distinct impression that he was asserting his authority, his claim to power, his right as a man to command me. I knew that I could do any job he set me to, and all I wanted was a chance. To get that chance, I had to surmount whatever obstacles were set in my way. If my being a woman was an obstacle, I would get around it by masking my difference from the men. I would not be called by a woman's name. I would adopt a name that was neutral.

"I'm B.J.," I told him, abbreviating Barbara Jean. I have been B.J. ever since.

"Well, B.J., we knew you would be coming out. Someone will show you to your room, then go to the galley and have lunch and report back here at noon."

Someone led me to another building, which was to be the

31

living quarters. The building struck me more as a storage area for papers and parts than a dormitory, though. I was shown the room where I would live and the bathroom, and then was left to settle my things in.

The room was narrow, barely nine feet wide, I guessed, with a single bed on either side. Although I had never lived in dormitories as a college student, this one struck me as like a dorm room. It definitely needed better lighting, and the institution-green paint was peeling in the corners. Still, it was clean. One bed was made up with clean linen and a blue blanket, the other with a flowered spread. A small table sat between the two beds, and bed lamps were attached to the walls. Tall lockers like those in a health club or high school were at the ends of the beds. I would have to bring some posters and a lamp in with me after my first week off to lend it some homeyness and comfort, but I never had been all that picky about interior decor. Next, I went to the bathroom, which was equipped with a two-head shower, two toilet stalls, and two washbasins with mirrors above. The ceramic tile gleamed, but it was as anonymous as an institution.

My stomach was rumbling, so I returned to the room and placed my folded jeans and workshirts on the shelves of the locker and my toilet articles in the drawers under the beds. I hadn't bothered to bring make-up; I'd figured that exaggerating my differences from my male co-workers was not the way to fit in. I quickly appraised my current outfit, the blue jeans and casual, long-sleeved shirt I had put on in New Orleans, and decided that I was ready for what came after lunch. By the end of the day, I had changed my mind about that.

The galley was a large, rectangular room with long, bright

orange tables at right angles to the wall. White molded chairs sat along them. Food was supplied to everyone working at East Bay as part of living there. The salad bar had cold cuts for sandwiches, and a steam table offered soups and hot foods. From the girth of some of the men munching hungrily at the tables there, the "eat all you want" policy was taken advantage of. I grabbed a salad and ham sandwich and sat down at a table with a few other men. No one was much interested in conversation. "You'll see when you get there," they said in answer to my questions. Their gruffness didn't offend me, though. I was familiar from the Air Force with that attitude toward new eager-beaver types. The old hands knew that experience was better than explanation anyway.

Still, back in Hoss's office after lunch, I felt out of place. Everyone was preoccupied. My determination to prove myself was forming into a desire to fit in. Hoss finally looked up from his desk as a man in red coveralls came in the door. "This is Lew," Hoss said. "You will be working in central facilities. He'll take you to the job. A gang is repairing a twenty-inch line that is broken. You'll help them."

Then he turned to Lew. "She'll need a hard hat and will work in Rob's gang. On the way, Champ."

I trailed along behind Lew. His face was a mess, covered with scabs as if he'd had dermabrasion surgery. I also noticed, along the jaw line tiny scars, like those from a facelift. He looked strong, with at least six feet of height and well-rounded quadriceps and biceps. We walked without his offering instructions or even a greeting.

Down some steps and along another metal grating catwalk over the muddy surface of the island, we came to the warehouse. The warehouseman, far more helpful and communicative than my escort, handed me the silvery aluminum hard hat. I felt a surge of elation, as if I had been handed a diploma or a key to the city. The warehouseman showed me how to assemble the headpiece and goggles on the hard hat. "If you need anything else, here's where you get it. We are supply central at East Bay."

Once more, Lew Pastee walked ahead of me out the warehouse door and along another catwalk. This time we walked behind the buildings I'd been in before and onto actual land rather than on the swampy soil I had been seeing. Lew pointed out a pickup truck and told me that we'd be taking it to the work site a mile down the oystershell road. As we drove he continued to hold his tongue. I curiously examined the equipment we passed, wishing he would offer explanations but too intimidated by his silence to ask for them. We passed a maze of pipelines and compressor stations with heavy machinery running. There were even many head of wild-looking cattle grazing along the bank.

We pulled up to where four or five men stood around a small mobile crane and a backhoe whose large claw had just scooped out a mountain of wet soil, making a crater fourteen feet deep and twenty feet wide. I followed Lew out of the truck and walked over to a fat balding man in overalls. Lew addressed him without introducing me: "Rob, this is your new hand."

"Hi, I'm B.J." And I stuck out my hand with a smile, hoping for a more friendly reception than I had met from the silent Lew. Rob shook my hand and got right to work. As what is called the "gang pusher," he had responsiblity for directing the team of workers on specific repair and maintenance projects. This gang was repairing a broken water line. The men had already dug out the line and were now fitting over it a split sleeve, a length of pipe split lengthwise, with bolts along the split that could be tightened down to make a cuff that would seal over the broken ends of the pipe.

Rob told me to climb down into the hole. As I started down the bank, I saw the two feet of water and felt the mud give under my feet. One other worker, who introduced himself as Nick, was already there. He was as dirty as he could be, and I was likely to look just like him soon. This was obviously a job for the low man—or in this case, woman—on the totem pole. But I had expected that I would have to prove myself, just like any other new worker. I was ready.

Using cable lines, the gang above lowered a power-driven impact wrench, a tool for loosening or tightening nuts, and a cable sling, to be looped around the pipe, to the two of us in the hole. My fingers struggled in the slippery goo, but I was able to connect the sling around the broken end of the pipe. The crane operator above was given the signal and lifted the broken ends of pipe above water level and even with each other. Nick and I fitted the sleeve over the break, and with the impact wrench I began tightening the nuts. Soon the job was complete.

I felt great, even though I was caked with rich Mississippi delta silt. This work with tools and equipment was familiar to me. I like the sense of achievement that comes with doing a job right. I enjoyed the muscular wrestling of the split sleeve into place. I knew that I would ache the next day, but I also knew that within a few weeks I would once again be in good condition, as I had been before I had worked as a nurse.

As Nick and I gathered up the tools and climbed out of the

crater, a cold January rain began to fall. The work had heated me up, so the downpour felt good. It also rinsed some of the mud from me. Nick and I took shelter under the crane.

For the first time, Nick started a conversation. "You have to be a whore or looking for a husband to be working out here."

The balloon of pleasure in the work, the sense of having completed a hard task side-by-side with this man, deflated with his bitter words.

"No, I'm neither of those," I said bluntly. "I'm already married. I've never sold sex but if I give it away, I consider it my business. I came here for a job, to earn a living, just like you did. I hope you don't have a problem with that."

"I'm the lead roustabout on the EB2," he warned, naming one of two main work barges that worked out of East Bay. "No one wants you to work there, and you are not welcome," Nick stated flatly.

"Fine. I hope I don't have to work there either, but if I do, I will do my best."

As I was staring at him, stunned by his resentment, another worker interrupted and introduced himself as Slade Mead, Nick's gang pusher. He congratulated us on a good job and sent us back to the quarters to clean up. I walked with Nick to the work boat at the edge of the bay, the Super Shell, and rode as he sullenly drove the boat to the quarters.

That boat ride offered me an opportunity to think more realistically than ever before about the social complexities that came with my new job. For the first time, I began to realize that not just Ervin Floyd, but many men didn't want me at East Bay, men with whom I would wrestle pipes and get dirty. Indeed, these men and I would reside together for seven days at a time. As eager for support, friendship, and acceptance as anyone else, I felt hurt by Nick's rejection. But I also knew how unfair his attitude was. I'd just proved myself to be capable, hard-working, and ready to do the dirty work, yet he hated me just because I'm a woman—how could such a thing be?

Back at the quarters I showered quickly and walked back to the Super Shell. Two work barges, the EB2 and the WSB1, were docked nearby. I heard with relief that I was assigned to the WSB1. That meant I wouldn't have to work with Nick and the others who he said did not want me there. Instead, I was assigned to the gang of Rob Smith, who directed the job I'd just completed. He already knew that I did a good job; maybe he would be on my side.

I was introduced to his lead roustabout, the second in command, Lloyd Larson. Lloyd showed me around the barge, pointing out equipment and giving instructions. He told me that I would learn to drive the barge to work locations, run the crane, and do welding. He explained different valves, tools, and fittings for piping. His communicative, friendly nature made me feel grateful and relieved. He also gave me my first assignment on the barge: I was responsible for looking over the engines every morning, checking the oil and water levels in the day tanks and the fluid levels in the welding machine. I also had to gather supplies from the warehouse for the day's work and put them aboard the jo-boat, the Supervisor III.

As he was finishing up instructions, another man came aboard the WSB1, a man Lloyd told me was Dick Samuels. Dick passed us without a word, not even acknowledging our presence. Lloyd told me that Dick had refused to work with or even be around me, so I wouldn't be allowed to assist him in any way. This was unfortunate for me, because I'd been a welder for years at General Motors. Why should one man's dislike of working with women keep me from a job I was already qualified to do?

The work crews spent most of the afternoon on the barges at the dock, cutting lengths of pipe in preparation for repairs the next day. I was shown around the EB2, a much larger barge than the WSB1. Forty-foot legs with gears cut into them could be dropped into the water even far off-shore, allowing the barge to actually be jacked up out of the water. The WSB1 had a similar feature, but it worked only in much shallower water. The equipment and procedures fascinated me, and I plagued Lloyd with questions.

Warmed by the January sun, I could tell that I would fall under the spell of this subtle landscape with its meandering canals. I felt a strange excitement when, at the end of the afternoon, the WSB1 pulled out to be dropped off at the location of the next day's repairs. Its slow motion down the narrow canal seemed graceful to me, if a work barge can be found graceful. I would really like this job, I thought, as I returned to my quarters for a shower before dinner. At least, I would if my co-workers would let me.

With great distress, though, I found out that evening how far the men of East Bay were determined to go to drive me away.

A movie theatre in the quarters offered nightly entertainment, so after dinner I decided to relax before a well-earned night's rest by enjoying one of my favorite John Wayne films. I walked into the darkened theatre, which already had about thirty people in it, and took my seat in an empty row, anticipating a pleasant two hours. Soon, someone sat down right beside me. "How odd," I thought, feeling wary and alert. I glanced out of the corner of my eye at the man. He was no one I had seen that day. I sat very still, in fact, hardly breathing, no longer able to concentrate on the movie.

In no more than a minute, he put his arm around the back of my chair. With surprise, I caught the odor of alcohol. I had been told that alcohol was strictly forbidden at East Bay, and yet this man seemed to have had plenty.

He leaned over and began to whisper, nearly choking me with the fumes from his breath. "Those other guys are afraid to do this, but I'm not." With that, he put his hand on my thigh and began to rub it up and down.

I was terrified, but rage also swept through me. I jumped up in front of everyone in the theatre as I gripped his arm in my angry fist. "If you ever touch me again, I'll kill you!" I shouted ferociously enough to drown out the gunfight on the screen. Everyone was watching me handle this confrontation; I realized with a jolt that I was being tested. I'd invaded the last male-only workplace in the country, and they were going to get me for it. They were inwardly cheering him on! Maybe they'd even set him up! As I turned to stride angrily up the aisle, I saw a sea of smirking faces illuminated dimly by the screen. The last thing I was to see as I left the theater, not to return for the next six months, was the malicious grin of Nick Claire.

Back in my room, I felt rejected, hurt, shaken, and enraged. I mulled over how angry some of the men of East Bay must be at my being hired. Some of them—Lloyd, Bill, and Padre, for example—had treated me decently, but others were hostile and unjust. How dare Nick call me a whore just because I wanted to do the same work and earn the same wages he did! Why did the gang pusher put up with Dick Samuels's refusal to work with me? Why did all the men in the theatre get a kick out of seeing that drunk put his arm around me? Could these men treat me so cruelly or watch me treated cruelly just because I was a woman? I'd heard the word "misogyny" defined as "the hatred of women" but always thought only sexual deviants and sociopaths were misogynists. Now I found myself in the midst of them. They were to be my co-workers and, perhaps even worse, my bosses!

Their attitude was so unfair to me. After all, Nick and I finished a job together. I pulled my share, did the work with only minimal directions, and didn't shrink from the difficulties. And yet he insulted me. Then Nick had already set himself against me before even seeing how well I could weld. They judged me without giving me a chance. Although I'd worked side-by-side with men in the Air Force, at General Motors, and at Michigan Bell, I'd never faced such anti-female bigotry before. I was beginning to understand that Ervin Floyd, the field superintendent at One Shell Square who had been so dead set against my being hired, was not the only one I'd have to prove myself to. That is, if these men were open-minded enough to let my hard work and excellent performance convince them they were wrong.

The drive to realize one's potential is an instinct, like hunger. A talent craves expression and growth. Unless unjustly suppressed, it will burst out as inevitably as a blossom in spring. In justice, society ought to encourage the blooming of individuals' talents.

Sexual harassment and discrimination are attempts to block a woman's instinctual drive for stability, acceptance, growth, and achievement. Rooted in prejudices about women's subordinate role, harassment and discrimination, like weeds, thwart women's stretch toward the sun.

Each of us whose aspirations and talents are being blocked owes it to herself to continue to move forward toward her own potential, even in the face of frustration. After all, who is to say what kind of work is meaningful work but the individual herself? The kind of work that repels one person attracts another.

3

HOW A WOMAN
OIL WORKER WAS BORN

✤

A strong sense of justice can help one cling to one's goals and aspirations. B.J.'s past taught her the importance of hard work and fair play. Her father's insistence that she could be anything she wanted to be taught B.J. to value her own potential. She brought this conviction with her to East Bay, and her sense of fairness helped her persist in trying to reach her goals even when Ervin Floyd attempted to refuse her the job with Shell Oil. Because of the ideals of justice that were her heritage, she knew that even though she was a woman, she had a right to any job she could do. And she was determined to win that right.

I was born in Harlan County in southeastern Kentucky on May 19, 1945, one of eight children raised off the scratch of the land. It was the kind of background celebrated in a lot of country music. In fact, an uncle of the Carters, the famous country western music family, lived in a shanty across the lane from our home. Sitting in the back yard in the late evenings, we could listen to the soft pull of the bow across his fiddle strings. Part of that basic American tradition, my parents believed in honesty and hard work. They taught us that we could be anything we wanted to be, and that the truth would stand when the world was on fire—and then they kept me and my brothers and sisters too busy with chores to learn anything else.

My parents married when my mom was about fourteen and my father was nineteen. They both grew up on farms on the rich soil of Somerset in southeastern Kentucky. Until World War II, they worked the land my mother inherited when her father died. Then the federal government gave my father a choice: be drafted or go work in the Kentucky coal mines to support the country's energy needs. With four children, he felt he had to become a miner, so he and mother moved the family to the mining area of Harlan County, and he worked in the coal mines for $1.11 ¾ an hour and held that job for the next twenty-eight years. Their fifth child, I was about eighteen months old at the time.

My mother at age fifteen gave birth to the first of her eight children at home, a daughter who weighed just two and a half pounds. The births spanned twenty-six years, the second child born six years after the first, and then one more every year and a half, until after another gap of ten years, the last two were born. My mother's mother lived with us the whole time, too, so my father's coal mining salary supported an entire family of eleven people.

All of us lived in a three-room converted barn. Two rooms were bedrooms with feather beds and cots, each with a coal-burning fireplace. The third room was a long kitchen with a sloped ceiling, containing a Home Comfort coal-burning cook stove with a warm water reservoir on the side. A long home-made table was surrounded with blasting powder boxes from the mines, which we kids used as chairs. We learned at an early age that if we kicked them while while we eating, we would earn a firm swat from our dad. The grownups sat on homemade hickory bottom chairs, which would be moved out onto the porch in the evenings.

Not that we sat peacefully on the porch much. I learned about hard work and independence from my family. We raised animals for food—chickens for Sunday dinner and hogs for smoked meat. Sometimes we had milk cows and other times bought milk for ten cents a gallon from neighbors. We canned food from our garden and orchard in half-gallon and gallon jars, sometimes putting up as many as 800 jars in a summer.

As a child I had the job of washing all those jars. I stood on the ground by the edge of the porch, on which sat two tubs filled at the household's water source, a spring 200 feet from the front door. The work was monotonous and seemed endless. Yet if I stopped paying attention as I moved the jars from the soapy tub to the rinse tub, the jar would slip out of my hands and break, and I would catch a scolding from Mom. I had to acquire self-discipline. Still, I was elated the summer when I discovered that my hand had grown too large to fit inside the mouth of the jars, certain that my younger sister would be recruited and I would be freed to learn something new. To my utter disappointment, my mother then just taught me how to do the canning.

Although I was the family cook from age seven on, I wasn't restricted to kitchen and household work. Perhaps this was because of my surprising size; I was always bigger than any other member of the family, even my brothers. Taking after my maternal grandfather, I grew to six feet one inch by the time I was in eighth grade. I was very thin, too. At graduation from high school in 1963, I weighed just 115 pounds. I couldn't even take advantage of my height by playing basketball, because in the early fifties in Kentucky, girls' basketball was against the law. So from the time I was a child, my physical size and my vigorous personality set me apart from everybody, even my sisters and brothers.

I worked at outdoor jobs along with my brothers for spending money. For instance, we could earn three cents a piece for cutting mining timbers with a cross-cut saw, a manual saw with a flat, one-edged blade about six feet long with a handle for a person at each end. The coal mine situated above our property used the timbers we cut to support the ceiling of its shaft. I cut mining timbers every day after school and during the summers from the time I was eight or nine years old. We could sometimes do a hundred a day. The mining company would come get them and pay us three dollars, which we split among us. It was hot, dirty, outdoor work. Still, I learned how to use the saw and how to keep it sharp. I also learned how to cooperate with my brothers.

This was just one of the chores that prepared me for blue-collar work, though. My brothers and I trapped and skinned animals. My father also used me as his assistant in building the smokehouse behind our home and taught me how to split hickory saplings to re-cane the bottoms of our homemade straight chairs.

My father was really the one who shaped my determination to get and hold the jobs I took on. He taught me that in a free country, hard work opens all doors.

I thought I was his favorite child. I'll admit, I was a tomboy, and my mother kept trying to make me into a lady, making me dresses I wouldn't wear. One day as she was giving me a whipping because I'd changed from one of my dresses into a pair of my brother's jeans, my father intervened. He laid down the law that I could wear what I wanted and that my mother should buy me clothes I could run around in the woods in. From that day on, she did. When my father got angry, there was trouble.

My whole family fought violently. We didn't just argue, we were out to kill—or at least maim. It was a battle royale, with all eleven of us having at one another. My sister once beat my father on the head with a shovel until she almost killed him; he bit her on the cheek, and she carried the scar to her grave. Those fights happened once a month or once every two months, often whenever my father had been drinking, which my mother didn't like. The battles would blow over entirely, though, and no one was badly hurt. I was certainly terrified, at times, but sometimes the worst in life can make a person stronger. At least, those brutal feuds hardened me for what I faced at Shell's East Bay.

My perceptions had been twisted, though, just as a battered wife loses the capacity to judge her assailant clearly.

After enduring years of ugly, threatening sexual harassment from workers at East Bay, I came to understand that I had somehow accepted the harassment as normal. Indeed, I became a part of it. My way of life as a child prepared me for that.

The rough, country way of life seemed to me as I grew up there completely normal, even a good life. I never knew that the world outside of our county existed. We had a radio and would listen to "Grand Ole' Opry" every Saturday night like almost everyone else in Harlan County, but we had no telephone or TV. Even school eight miles away in Cumberland, Kentucky, didn't bring us into the wider world. We who lived in the country were called "river rats" by the town students because the busses took us up the river; they kept themselves aloof from us.

Still, all of the Poynter children did well in school. Our parents insisted that we make good grades, be respectful to our teachers, and attend classes whether we were sick or not. Cumberland High School graduated 112 students in 1963, and I was one of them. Since I'd earned high grades, especially in the science classes, I won a semester's scholarship at a branch of the University of Kentucky. I was absolutely thrilled at this opportunity. I knew that scholarships and my own earning power were the only ways to fulfill my dream of going to college, because my father's health was debilitated by black lung disease, caused by breathing coal dust in the mines. Three other children were still in school. No financial help was forthcoming from my family.

But the struggle to fund my own education was unsuccessful. I spent the summer with an older sister in northern Indiana, hoping to earn enough money working first in a hamburger stand and then as a nurse's aide at the county hospital, so the science and technology that had so fascinated me in high school was applied in a hospital. I loved learning about the equipment, the tests, and the chemistry, which nurses understood.

Unfortunately, after a successful semester at the university, I was forced to withdraw: I was out of money, my father was even more ill, and the family needed whatever I could contribute. I moved to Dumas, Arkansas, to live with another sister and brother-in-law and my five nieces and nephews and got another nurse's aide job, which brought me in touch with the good people of Desha County, Arkansas.

There I saw prejudice in action for the first time, for the black patients were hospitalized in a separate ward. I sometimes went to help the black nursing assistant assigned to that ward when my work was caught up. My father always told me, "there's no need to treat colored people differently. They're human, just like you." Yet, since no people of color had lived in the mountain region of Harlan County, I hadn't had the privilege of their friendship before. Just less than six months out of high school, I was still inexperienced. I'd never understood how unkindness and bigotry can actually be built into a system, like a medical care system. Unluckily, by the time I took on oil production labor as a woman at Shell Oil, I had forgotten this lesson.

My sister died unexpectedly—even an autopsy could not discover the cause—so I returned to my other sister in Indiana, this time with an older brother. Once again I went to work at the hamburger stand, earning just $1.25 an hour. My brother, however, was able to find work at a local factory for a much better salary. I envied him, as my dreams for college seemed even further and further away. A few months later, in January of 1965, he wrangled me an interview that was to introduce me to a line of work women ordinarily didn't hold. I was just twenty years old at the time, but the interview changed my life.

An electrical manufacturing company was looking for a warehouseman or storekeeper. The job entailed lifting and stacking boxes of equipment sometimes weighing as much as 200 pounds, using manual hand trucks and lifts. The plant manager whom I met in the warehouse took one skeptical look at my six-foot, one inch height and skinny frame and decided to give me a strength test. He pointed out a box of parts three feet by three feet by three feet that was heavier than I was. A manual hand-truck lift stood nearby. He instructed me to get that box and stack it on the top of four other boxes twenty feet away. I was supposed to slide the box onto the fork of the hand truck as it sat on the floor. I tried and tried, but couldn't seem to get the flat metal base of the hand truck to go under the box's bottom.

I began to feel anxious. I wanted the job badly. The higher salary meant more money, enough to attend night classes at the town's branch campus of Purdue University. Only one solution seemed available. I stepped away from the fork lift controls, squatted down with my hips low, and actually lifted the box onto the fork lift. Standing up again, I looked at the plant manager's amazed face. He hadn't expected a skinny girl to be able to do what few of his warehousemen even tried to do. "You're hired," he said immediately.

Soon I was making more money than I ever dreamed possible and could afford to send money home, rent my own apartment, buy my first used car—a '57 Chevy—and take night classes. Concentrating on school after a day's labor at the factory wasn't easy, but I was able to accumulate hours towards my college degree. Taking just one or two classes a semester, though, I was going to take forever to get a degree. In 1971, after six years of work at the electrical manufacturing firm, I realized that with the country at war and the G.I. Bill available to veterans, I could speed up the process. I joined the Air Force and became a medic.

After basic training, I was sent to the Air Force Medical School in Texas. There I trained in field and emergency medicine. I learned to suture lacerations, perform various minor surgical operations, pump stomachs, administer intravenous fluids, and offer many other life-saving aids. Later, the Air Force assigned me to Homestead Air Force Base in Homestead, Florida, where I worked in the emergency room and walk-in clinic, two of the busiest departments in the hospital. The colonel who wrote the letter recommending that I be sent to a special physician's assistant's program said that I was a "natural leader" who "performed brilliantly in life-threatening situations." I had my own office and saw patients, did my own X-rays and dispensed drugs, wrote prescriptions for physicians' signature, admitted patients to the hospital, and did minor surgeries for doctors. I got out of the Air Force two years early to attend physician's assistant's school.

That requires four years of medical school. Western Michigan and a school in Lincoln, Nebraska, were the only schools in the country to offer a Physician's Assistant program, so I applied to go to Western Michigan. The college took only twenty-five students a year. When I got there, I was told that my transcripts from the University of Kentucky had been lost, and the administration wouldn't let me hand-carry another copy. So I didn't get in that year.

There I was in Kalamazoo. I took a temporary job with

Michigan Bell as a telephone installer, my second non-traditional job and one that my work in the electrical manufacturing warehouse had prepared me for. In the early seventies, people weren't used to seeing a woman climbing telephone poles. I liked the work, though, and Michigan Bell liked me so much that the company wanted me to stay on permanently. I went instead to the nursing program at Kalamazoo Valley College, thinking that nursing would be much the same kind of work as I had been doing as a medic in the Air Force.

That wasn't at all the case, though, and I got into trouble because I was so much more seasoned than the typical nursing student. For example, my instructor was shocked when I didn't fall apart at the death of a patient I'd been assigned. The patient had advanced kidney cancer, renal carcinoma. Although he was hospitalized, no one thought he was in critical condition. Certainly, a student nurse wouldn't have been assigned to care for him if his death was expected.

One morning I got him out of bed, fed him his breakfast, administered his medicine, and helped him dress. I also repeatedly checked his blood pressure. It just kept dropping. However, I wasn't overly concerned because I knew that was typical of renal problems, and the steady flow of urine from his catheter showed that the kidneys were still working. Suddenly, about mid-morning, the patient went into shock. Luckily, I was in his room to notice it and tossed a bedpan clattering out into the hallway to get the attention of the staff nurses. They didn't want a student handling emergencies because insurance didn't cover us.

As the patient was being cared for by the staff, the nursing instructor took me into the supply room, very upset that the emergency had occurred.

"There was nothing I could do about it," I told her. "The man was very ill and is doomed to die."

"I'm going to sent you to the school psychologist," she said, "because you're not handling this right."

"I have seen more people die than you have," I told her, and began to tell her of the emergencies I had handled in the Air Force. I had learned to accept that death takes some patients in spite of our best efforts, as most medical people do after years of seasoning. My instructor, who was used to more emotion from her inexperienced students, determined that I see a psychologist and told me that I would never pass her class. By the end of the semester, however, she came to realize that I'd been telling her the truth.

A hospital refused my application for a nurse's aide position for a similar reason. "If we were to hire you," they said, "the time would come when you would overstep your bounds, and our insurance would not cover you." So, unable to find work to support myself during school, I joined the Michigan Air National Guard and completed my degree on the G.I. bill. I took every biology, chemisry, and physics course offered, simply because I was interested in it, and ended up with an Associate of Science degree.

My job at an open-heart unit in Kalamazoo, Michigan, didn't command a high enough salary to support me and my husband while he took his turn at college, though. I'd met Joseph Holcombe while he and I were on active duty in the Air Force. He'd come with me to Michigan for Physician's Assistant's training and taken a job at the Michigan Air National Guard base as a member of the Air National Guard, as I did while I got my degree. Now that I was done, he wanted the opportunity for an education. So once again I went to a non-traditional job in search of the salary women couldn't draw. I was hired by General Motors as a welder on an automobile assembly line. Although the work required strength and endurance, the rewards were ample for our needs. While Joe got his degree in machine tool technology, we together bought and remodeled a house, which we were able to sell at a healthy profit.

Our college degree goals realized and with extra cash in our pockets, we headed for the warmer climate of northwestern Florida, where we'd been stationed temporarily by the Air Force, me to earn a Florida nursing license and Joe to work as a civilian for the Navy. That's when my own impatience with nursing's low pay finally led me to the doorsteps of One Shell Square.

✧

B.J.'s family heritage reflected that basic American promise that all people will be treated equally. Rugged though her upbringing was, she was able to grow up believing that her individual talents were more important to her success than her sex, her race, or any social category she fit into.

B.J.'s father taught her that her success was bounded only by her aspirations. But social customs that assign work to women or to men threatened to strangle her aspiration.

Only those who aspire to a goal outside the borders of social custom will discover, as B.J. did, the boundaries of freedom

III
HARDSHIP

❧

Why should women face job hazards and job requirements men are not expected to face?

That's what is happening when bosses demand more of us on the job than is asked of men, and when, in order to gain acceptance, we accept the assumption that we must be better workers than men.

We may also face other hazards men don't have to confront, like harassment by employees of the other sex and lack of support by our life partners.

Justice to women demands that their path of employment success be free of the special hazards to them that men may never encounter.

work gang, Gang Pusher Rob Smith, Welder Dick Samuels, and Lead Roustabout Lloyd Larson. My position was Maintenance Man C-new, even though I am a woman. I found out later that no worker other than me had ever been classified as "new." The classification was invented just for me, and it stuck even after two years. They evidently didn't expect me to last.

The gangs themselves were ordinarily composed of the boss, called the gang pusher, a welder or other specialist, and several other workers, called roustabouts, one of whom would be the "lead" roustabout. Seniority and experience determined where a person stood in the pecking order. I knew that it was my job to keep my eyes open, do my work well, and watch my step to avoid aggravating the touchy situation I found myself in.

We were to be joined by other workers later. They were contract hands, not official employees of Shell Oil, but supplied by a local contractor out of New Orleans. Like regular Shell employees, they too lived on location all week long. In fact, the East Bay living quarters ordinarily housed about seventy-five Shell and a hundred contract employees for their week-long hitches. Each week the crew would alternate with the other week-long crew, the "A" and the "B" crews, and each crew felt a bit of team rivalry toward the other crew.

Gang Pusher Rob gave us our tasks. We were to load supplies from the warehouse onto the job boat, which everyone pronounced "jo-boat," and go out to a well jacket where some repairs to valves and supporting structures had to be made. A well jacket is actually an oil well. I had seen one, a Chevron Oil Company well jacket, on the boat ride from the terminal the day before. The work barge, the WSB1, which was equipped with a welding machine, a crane, and a supply of long pipes, was already out there. Rob sent us to the warehouse to collect flanges, bolts, gaskets, and other supplies. I was also sent to fill up the large, insulated water bucket with water and ice for the day's work. It was a simple job, but I knew that as the new worker I would be assigned the lowliest tasks. That's the way a pecking order works.

Once loaded up, we climbed in the thirty-five-foot jo-boat and took off along the calm canal. We sat inside the small cabin of the jo-boat, Rob at the helm and the rest of us facing one another on the two padded benches. As I settled in for the ride, I sized up my fellow work gang members. Rob was a heavy man, much overweight. His thinning hair suggested that he might be around forty. He seemed pleasant enough, with his "Proud Father" T-shirt and genial manner. I later learned that he was indeed a family man; his wife and he were about to adopt their second child. Dick the welder still had not glanced my way; his anger was chilling me, so I looked away. Lloyd struck me as being much younger than I was, but I learned later that he and I were the same age, thirty-four. A black man, he seemed more sympathetic to my being at East Bay than anyone I had yet met. Perhaps that was because black workers hadn't been hired by Shell Oil until the early seventies.

After we were well underway, Rob asked Lloyd if he'd checked the jo-boat's oil and water levels before leaving. Lloyd said, "I'll get to it when we get to the barge." Since Lloyd had told me that these jobs would be my responsibility, I hopped to those simple tasks as soon as we docked alongside the barge moored to the well jacket. I climbed down the ladder into the bilge, the empty hull area under the deck, ducking my head considerably to fit into mere five-and-a-half foot clearance. I walked along the narrow metal grating catwalk made slippery by the oily six or eight inches of water sloshing around in the bilge. I would have to take care of pumping that out later. With my flashlight I found the two large, Detroit-built V-8 engines that sat near the back end and began to check the oil level. Just as you check the oil level on a car engine, I read the level with a metal stick that rests in the oil chamber of the engine. I also checked the water level in the day tank, which was the engine's cooling system. I then turned my attention to the water sloshing in the bilge. Evidently, the WSB1's hull leaked, and the oil in the water suggested as well that the engines were throwing off oil as they ran.

My previous work experience and life experiences around boats taught me that a pump is usually set up to empty the bilge, so I began tracing pipelines that looked as if they were used to evacuate the excess water. Eventually, I found the bilge pump that operated off the Number One engine and then traced the discharge line. If I were to start the pump engine to empty the bilge, then the dirty, oily water inside the bilge would get dumped right into the bay, and I knew that that would pollute the water, so I decided to ask Lloyd what to do.

I found him and Rob busy with the jo-boat engine and told them the problem. Rob explained that the usual process was to pour degreaser into the bilge, which would disperse and dissolve the oil, and then discharge it into the bay.

"What? Have you never heard of pollution laws?" I exclaimed.

"Well," said Rob, with a smile at my greenness, "when we're still at the quarters, we are supposed to discharge the bilge water into a drain hooked up to a contained system, but out here this is the way we have always done it."

Meanwhile, Lloyd had already put degreaser into the jo-boat bilge and was pumping the water overboard. The foamy discharge floated on top of the muddy canal water. I didn't like it.

"It really don't hurt nothing," Lloyd said apologetically.

"Wouldn't it be easier and safer to locate the leaks on the vessels and repair them so it wouldn't be necessary to pollute?" I asked. I would do what was expected of me, but I made a promise to myself to find the suggestion box, wherever the company had it, and stop the unnecessary and thoughtless spoiling of the bay, if I could.

Next, I turned to the welding machine, which Lloyd had also said would be my responsibility. This equipment was familiar territory because of my welding experience on the car assembly lines at General Motors. I checked out the fuel tank and oil tank and added to each. They were ready. With a feeling of satisfaction at this beginning, I went over to Rob for further direction.

He'd seen me at the welding equipment, and he repeated what Lloyd had told me the afternoon before.

"You're not to help the welder at all. When he gets used to your being here, you will be able to work with him. Right now, though, get on the well jacket and disconnect the flowline. The well is already shut in, but just check to make sure."

He pointed to the well jacket, the two-inch yellow pipes and stack of valves called a "Christmas tree." It stood in the water, surrounded by a narrow metal grating platform. I was soon to become very familiar with this structure, but at that time my talent for mechanical things told me what I needed to do. The pipelines running into it were obviously the flow lines. I could tell that I would need open-end box end wrenches to fit over the bolt heads and a hammer wrench to loosen the three-inch bolts, which had been badly corroded by the salt water. I would need a small sledge hammer to pound the end of the wrench. It was the same principle as loosening the lug nuts on a car's wheel.

The rest of the gang went about their jobs while I followed Rob's instructions. I knew he was watching me work out of the corner of his eye. I checked the master valve and the flow line valves to make sure they were in the "off" position, blocking the flow of crude oil to the pipe joint that needed repair. Then I picked up an empty bucket, gathered my wrenches, gaskets, studs, and other tools in it, and walked over to the leaking joint. My task was to break loose the bolts that held the pipe ends together, so as to disconnect the lines. I settled the wrenches over each bolt, gave the hammer wrench two or three firm blows with the sledge hammer, and then moved on to the next. When each bolt was loose enough, I began to work around the joint with my wrench until all the old bolts were out. I worked the pipe ends loose from one another. Then I replaced the leaking pipe with the new piece that had been cut the day before. The job was complete, and Rob nodded his approval.

Musing while I wiped off and replaced my tools, I felt proud and fulfilled. Using those tools and working with that equipment, I had the uncanny sensation that I'd been somewhere like East Bay before. It was as if I already knew how to do the work I was being asked to do. Perhaps I'd simply found work ideally suited to my native talents. How fortunate I was, I thought. A woman's mechanical talents aren't often recognized and developed in this society. I'd ended up a nurse, a traditionally "feminine" job, after all. If I hadn't impulsively filled out that job application Joe had brought home, I'd never have found work that seemed to suit me so well.

With a grin, I reported to Rob for my next assignment. We were to repair a weakened angle iron and to replace some grating on the walkway that had rusted through. Both these tasks required the welder.

Lloyd went to the barge and picked up the cutting torch to carry to the structure. I unwound the hose from the oxygen and acetylene tanks and followed Lloyd to make sure that they didn't snag on equipment. The safety of the welder and anyone else in the vicinity depended on keeping the explosive gasses well contained and away from sparks that might ignite them. Using the welding torch, Dick cut the grating loose and the rusty angle iron as well. To my surprise, he simply tossed these metal pieces into the water. Wasn't that pollution, or at least littering, as well?

The rough edges left by the cutting torch had to be smoothed before a weld could be made to complete the repairs. I moved in with the chipping hammer which was used to knock off the excess metal from the edges. As I began, Dick turned abruptly away and walked off the structure onto the barge and stayed there until the next step, the welding, was to begin. He never said a word to me.

He came back and began to make the weld. "Lloyd, hand me a stud to two-hole this flange," he said. Without thinking, I picked up the bolt he had asked for from the storage bin right next to me. "Here," I said, handing it to him.

He reached out his hand, took the stud, and threw it overboard. "Lloyd," he barked, "I asked for a stud."

Rob, Lloyd and I exchanged glances, but no one spoke, and Dick proceeded with the weld.

A call on the intercom announced that the contract hands who were expected were on the dock waiting to be picked up.

"B.J., come with me," Rob said.

"OK." I rose and moved to untie the boat.

On the way, Rob was reasssuring. "Don't pay any attention to Dick. He will get used to you and things will be all right. I can tell by the way you are working that you have experience. Things will work out."

I was grateful for his support, but I was also distressed by Dick. "It's OK," I said to Rob, trying to be as cooperative as I could. "I'm just not used to people acting this way. I don't understand it."

"I want you to know something. Your not being allowed to help the welder or do some other jobs you're qualified to do was not my idea. The orders come from higher up."

"You mean from God?" I asked sarcastically. I was shocked by what Rob was telling me. Was I in Russia, I thought, that someone could keep me from doing work I was qualified to do? Was there some kind of conspiracy against me? Then Ervin Floyd's promise rang again in my ears: "I will do whatever is necessary to keep you out of East Bay." I got curious.

"Who made this decision for you? I should think that as my boss, you would have the right to decide what work I would and would not do."

"I can't tell you that," replied Rob, turning his eyes away from me to the canal ahead. "But I will tell you it was not a decision from anybody in the field. It came from someone higher."

My suspicions of Ervin Floyd deepened. No one at East Bay, but someone at One Shell Square, had blocked my opportunities. I thought I'd be able to prove myself and fit in.

Perhaps that wasn't the case, I thought for the first time in my life.

Rob went on. "When we heard you were coming out here, some men just made up their minds that they wouldn't work with a woman. They never have before. They feel it is no place for a woman to work. Women are supposed to be at home. Their wives either don't work, or they work in offices."

I nodded. I knew many of the people in this part of the country had run their households according to those rules. But I'd been in Michigan's auto industry, where, like many other industries, men and women both work at manual labor and think nothing of it. I simply hadn't expected discrimination to run this deep. And I hadn't anticipated being the person to have to run the gauntlet.

"Personally," continued Rob, "I like having you on my gang, and I can tell that you will get along fine. But lots of rumors are going around about you."

I snorted in agreement, thinking of Nick's accusation that I must be a whore or out for a husband. "Well, I'm not interested in rumors," I said with some bitterness. "I just want to do a good job and get paid. I've never worked where people treated me like this."

Rob explained that I would probably work on his gang for only a few weeks and then be moved to the other barge, the EB2, with Slade Mead as supervisor. I was to be shifted from one gang to another to give me a broad perspective of the field and allow the men to get used to working with me.

It sounded to me like I was to be a guinea pig, but I kept my thoughts to myself. We were approaching the dock where the contract workers were milling in a small group. "Well," I told myself, "I'll just stick it out. I have always been tough."

As we landed, I took the boat's tie, wrapped it around the dock's piling, and gave it an especially strong tug.

Rob and I and the new contract workers returned to the well where the WSB1 work barge was moored and began to work in two teams. I and the other roustabouts reconnected the repaired flow line and gas lift lines while Lloyd worked with Dick to weld the new grating into place. When we were done, Rob called the well's lease operator, the worker responsible for inspecting the well and reporting production rates and repair needs to the field supervisor. The lease operator was on the platform into which the crude oil from this well ran. I heard his nasal voice over the shortwave radio thanking us and giving instructions. "The well is lined up at the platform. Go ahead and open it up and open the gas, too. I'll come by and set it later and check it out."

We turned the valve handles, which look like steering wheels, as if we were taking a broad left turn. I could hear the crude oil flow whooshing through the two-inch pipes.

"Pretty neat," I thought to myself with a grin. "I've just helped put my first oil well back into production." I turned to Rob. "What does the crude oil look like coming out of the well?"

He snatched up a bucket and thrust it at me. "Take this and crack the needle valve on the flowline and catch some in it."

I did. It was foamy and brown, with the strong, familiar odor of oil. It was thinner than the oil I was used to pouring into my car. I learned later, though, that the crude oil coming from individual wells varies. As it sat, the oil separated from the water and floated, becoming even darker brown. This was the liquid that fueled the country—in fact, the world. And I was helping produce it. Again, I felt a grin coming on.

We were picking up tools and equipment and boarding the barge for our next assignment when Rob called out the lunch break. Everybody moved to grab a brown bag that the cook at the quarters had packed the night before. Everybody, that is, except Lloyd, who had brought himself a steak from somewhere and was cooking it on a two-burner stove in the barge's cabin. I sniffed the aroma of sauteed meat as I munched my tuna fish and carrots.

Rob and I sat on the benches inside the cabin while the contract workers perched here and there on the deck of the barge. Dick took his bag and moved onto the jo-boat. I'd been hoping he and I would get acquainted and discuss differences.

"Why did the welder leave?" I asked Rob.

"You're sitting in his spot," he grunted.

I scrutinized Dick as he sat there alone on the boat in the sun. He certainly wasn't as mature and dignified as he looked. His medium build, silver-grey hair, and Van Dyke beard streaked with auburn made him look really distinguished. His very blue eyes reminded me of Paul Newman, but there was none of the mischievous twinkle and warmth in Dick's eyes that made Paul's so appealing. And his attitude certainly seemed childish. Later I learned that people's seats for lunch were part of the pecking order, too: the contract workers sat in separate locations to signal their difference from the Shell-hired workers.

While we ate, Lloyd told me more about my job. He would teach me to drive the barge, operate the pedestal crane that sat on it, and maintain the barge itself. I would soon be lead roustabout in that crew, he told me. He was pleased to be training his replacement, because as Maintenance Man A he was next in line for promotion to one of the speciality positions, which meant higher pay and less rigorous duties. For my part, I felt nervous at the sudden responsibility. How could they expect me to learn all this new work so rapidly? Perhaps this was how Floyd planned to get rid of me—by throwing so much at me so fast that I would fail. Lloyd didn't seem to notice my uneasiness, though.

Here and there, the gang members were climbing to their feet, hitching up their work pants, and tossing their wadded lunch garbage overboard. More littering, I noticed. Rob directed me to help Lloyd to take the barge over to the next worksite, an actual oil platform, while the rest of the gang and contract workers rode over on the boat.

Lloyd led me to the cabin, which sat at the very rear of the fifty-foot flat-bottomed barge. From the cabin I could look over all the equipment on the deck, including the pedestal crane and the array of pipes of various diameters. On each side of the barge were long, heavy vertical legs, called "spuds," which could be lowered into the mud under the shallow water of the bay, turning the barge into a stable, standing platform.

The cabin itself had a big two-and-a-half foot wheel that controlled the rudders of the barge. It stood in front of a control panel with meters, and on either side were levers that were the clutches for each of the two engines. Lloyd began to show me how to drive the whale of a boat. As he patiently pointed out each control and explained what I was to do, I visualized the functions taking place. I put the clutch lever into a neutral position and pushed the start button, and a low rumble burst from the engine area below and behind me. Then I slowly moved the hydraulic lever to raise the "spuds," allowing us to float free. I moved the clutch position to reverse, as Lloyd instructed, and that drew us slowly into open water. Then he had me move the clutch into forward, and the barge's backward momentum slowed, stopped and reversed into forward movement, all in slow motion. By throttling the two engines on either side of the barge to different speeds, I could actually turn the barge without steering it.

I stood behind the large steering wheel looking forward through the huge pedestal crane on the forward deck and felt a surge of excitement. Lloyd seemed to feel it, too.

"You're the first woman in the world ever to drive this barge."

He was right. I might not be the first American woman in space, but I was a Sally Ride in my own right. I was a woman working in the oil fields, a place supposed to be too tough for women. I was a woman who could understand and handle heavy equipment, and not only that, I was getting an enormous kick out of it. I was a woman who was driving a massive, slow-moving dinosaur of a boat and doing it perfectly competently. When Lloyd said, "You'll get the hang of it," I nodded confidently. I felt good.

We were headed to Platform A, where a leak on a manifold, a series of valves that directed various components of the crude oil to separate locations, needed repair. The route to the location took us through a maze of canals that had been dredged out of the marshlands for barge passage. "How will I ever find my way around all these?" I wondered. "I can't drop crumbs behind me like Hansel and Gretel." Not knowing the canals' depth, I kept to the middle. Even though I was concentrating on not grounding the barge, I was still able to enjoy our slow, stately passage through the subtle scenery. Clumps of a tall reed that Lloyd called "roso" grew thick and lush along the banks. Many ducks and other water fowl paddled between them, ignoring us. No trees grew here, only grasses and some low bushes rooted in the rich mud and mildly saline water of the Mississippi delta.

As we turned into another canal, the sea quickened and waves rocked the barge. We seemed to be emerging from marsh to the actual edge of the bay. After a short radio conversation with Rob, who was already at Platform A with the rest of the work gang, Lloyd took over the controls to pilot the barge through these new difficulties. I stepped aside with satisfaction, eager to see the open waters ahead.

Over the next years, the sailing was far from free, though. I felt thrills of exhilaration at being the first woman to work Shell's East Bay, as well as hurt and anger at men's hateful behavior toward me. I learned that being the first woman in a male-dominated workplace is like storming a fortress and catching the first fire, to use metaphors from some of my favorite John Wayne films. I'd neither expected nor wanted such a responsibility; all I'd wanted was a good job with good wages. I'd assumed that if I could do the work well, I'd be treated fairly and respectfully. I wasn't.

The patterns called "gender-based harassment" and "sexual harassment" were clear.

Gender-based harassment involves discrimination in work assignments, promotions, work conditions, and other circumstances of the job. In all sorts of ways, my bosses and co-workers manipulated my work environment just because they didn't like having me, a woman, at East Bay. My first-day assignment to the work gang on WSB1 was just one example of gender-based harassment. Although I didn't realize it at the time, I later learned that my original assignment was to Central Facilities, but it had been changed because the supervisor of that division refused to accept me as a worker. He announced to the Operations Foremen that "he would trade me for the laziest, worst worker they had." So while I might have ended up with warehouse work, instead I went to a work gang that worked mostly in the marshes—the hottest, hardest, lowest job at East Bay. Perhaps the bosses were following Ervin Floyd's directions to drive me out. I didn't run from hard work, though. I like to sweat.

Ervin Floyd continued to try to influence my work assignments and evaluations. He frequently called the Operations Foreman to find out if I'd been driven away yet. One day I was in the foreman's office when Ervin Floyd's call came through. The foreman held the telephone up to my ear so that I could hear for myself Floyd's angry threats. I appreciated that.

But discrimination against me by individuals was just one aspect of the gender-based harassment I experienced over the next eight-and-a-half years. Another problem was that one raised by Phyllis Schlafly in her fight against the Equal Rights Amendment: Shell Oil's policy about toilet facilities. It was indeed a problem for me, as any woman who has been on a boat with men can well imagine.

Except when they were at the living quarters, the men of East Bay defecated and urinated directly into the open water from the boats, barges, and platforms. The men who disliked having a woman as a co-worker often urinated near me, hoping to embarass me. At some platforms, toilet seats even hung over the water from catwalks for the convenience of the lease op-

71

erators, who spent much of their time on them. This assault on the water's purity was directly contrary to Coast Guard regulations, but the company itself promoted the practice by giving the men no alternative. Once we left the living quarters on the barrier island for our workday on the water and in the marshes, there was nowhere else to go.

Because the company seemed so indifferent to the polluting of the Gulf with human wastes, the workers themselves were unconcerned, too. Once a co-worker of mine—his name was D.J.—actually dumped a bucket into which he had just defecated while the Coast Guard was inspecting the platform we were working on. D.J. had simply forgotten that dumping untreated human wastes into open water was against Coast Guard regulations. After all, it was standard operating procedure. But the Coast Guard saw D.J. do it, and it was rumored that the company was fined $5,000. Among the crew working East Bay, it became a joke, a laugh that he had been caught.

But I wasn't laughing. Like everyone else, I was forced into polluting the Gulf, but unlike everyone else, I couldn't just turn my back, unzip my pants, and let myself go. Having to hold it was uncomfortable and unhealthy for me as well. My childhood kidney and bladder infections had left my kidneys scarred. In spite of this medical history, on workdays spent on jo-boats, well jackets, and platforms I was often forced to do without relief for almost twelve hours. I wasn't about to bare my behind in front of men already too aware that I was different from them. On the days when the work barge was available, I was able to go down into the bilge for privacy. A bucket, crassly labelled "B.J.," was given to me to use. Every time I grabbed it and took it down into the barge's bilge, I felt the men's eyes on me and felt embarassed.

The company should provide toilet facilities for us, I thought. After all, I *was* built different from the men, and so my basic human need to relieve myself had to be dealt with differently. Since the company had assigned me separate sleeping quarters, it recognized my need for privacy, at least while on the island. Why not put port-o-lets on the platforms, I asked my boss? That way, all of us would be in fairly easy boating distance wherever we were working.

I made my suggestion to my supervisor. His response was one I would become used to: "Don't be a troublemaker. If you don't like the way things are, lots of people are waiting to get your job. Pack up your clothes and go to the bank." "The bank" was a way of saying "final paycheck." So, when I complained about the lack of bathroom facilities, I was threatened with being fired.

The threat that I would be fired certainly stopped me in my tracks. Besides liking and needing the job, I, like most people, took pride in my excellent work record. I wouldn't want to have to explain to a prospective employer why I was dismissed from Shell Oil.

Yet I felt frustrated at my supervisor's resistance. Surely, I should have a right to make suggestions and point out problems in the way the company operated. Where could I go with my suggestion? Should I protest these threats, and how? Few companies tell their employees how to file a complaint or a grievance. A good source of information may be the union steward, but unfortunately for me and many other workers with problems, Shell was a non-union shop. In other words, the fox was in charge of the henhouse. As I look back on these first few years at East Bay, I realize that I was incredibly naive. I simply did not understand how I might stand up for myself.

73

I didn't know how to file a gender-based harassment complaint. And I had no one to ask.

And if I made the effort to claim my right to toilet facilities, if I kept lodging complaints until they fired me, wouldn't that be giving them just the opportunity to fire me that they wanted? Wasn't this just a way of driving me out of East Bay? I felt that I had to just hold it, uncomfortable as I was, for my own sake and for other women who might want to work at East Bay.

Thus my simple need for toilet facilities began a moral crisis for me, you might say. I either had to fight the injustice directly, and so jeopardize my job, or stick with it in hopes of changing Shell's policies and my co-workers' practices.

I chose to stick with it, and the legacy of that decision is guilt. I became an accomplice in the company's discrimination against women, as I see it now. When I first came to East Bay, more than anything I wanted to fit in. I thought that if I didn't make waves, the supervisors would see me as "easy to work with" and "able to get along with others." That would pave the path to promotions. By pursuing the company's high pay without challenging the company's practices, I accepted the discriminatory system. Ambition had corrupted me as well.

I began to work especially hard to prove myself to the supervisors who evaluated me. I accepted without protest physically demanding assignments designed to exhaust me. In one case, I and another co-worker were told to move a large pile of very heavy pipes from one part of the barge to another— by hand. Each pipe was thirty feet long and very heavy. Normally, the pipes would have been banded together and lifted in a bunch by means of a crane. But the boss wanted it done by hand, and I would do it. I carried two-hundred-pound loads of pipe and valves on my back through snake-infested swamp. Once I even stood in chest-high water holding a piling upright with my arms while a pile-driving machine pounded it in just above my head.

My willingness to accept physically challenging tasks did win me some respect. My gang pusher's weekly evaluations noted that I gave a hundred fifty percent, and a lease operator who saw me holding the piling while it was being driven congratulated me on my good work. In fact, I became known as "a good worker." I took on these tasks willingly, relishing the sensations of exhaustion I felt at the end of a day of hard work. And I hoped to change the minds of the men who worked at East Bay.

B.J. made a personal commitment to herself to work at a very high level of excellence. She wanted to prove to the gender terrorists among her fellow workers that women could do "men's work" as well as—or even better than—many men. By setting her own standards of performance and then meeting them, she gave herself a personal, independent basis for self-esteem.

Nevertheless, a woman ought not to have to be a "Superwoman" in order to hold a job and to work free of discrimination and harassment. Instead, a woman should have the same right to perform at every level of achievement that men do—all the way from mediocre to excellent—without its being taken as proof that women can't do the work.

B.J. was trying to prove to the men who discriminated against her that there is no "men's work" and no "women's work" but only work that some men can do better than some women and vice versa. Our society will have achieved equality when no woman has to personally shoulder the burden of representing her entire sex.

5

A PERVERT ON A BOAT

ⴽⵯⵓ

B.J. was sexually harassed by a co-worker who continually displayed his genitals to her whenever he could get her alone. He also tried to embarrass her with explicit sexual talk and behavior. To his dismay, his perverted behavior did not have the effect that he intended. Having been a medic, B.J. was not as easily shocked by his sexual displays as someone else might have been. She also understood that when someone ridicules or tries to shame or humiliate a person because of her sexual characteristics or any other aspect of herself, that person is revealing his own uneasiness. Calling a pervert a pervert, she focused the shame back on the gender terrorist.

B.J. was able to insulate herself from her co-worker's attempt to shame or humiliate her by holding him responsible for his own attitudes rather than adopting them by feeling shame. She did feel isolated, though, and she trusted few people with the story of the pervert on the boat. That isolation was perhaps more damaging than the disgust she felt for the pervert.

❧ For two years, I had been a Maintenance Man B working in work gangs. By this time I should have been promoted to Maintenance Man A, with its increase in pay, but I hadn't been. This was especially annoying to me because I'd worked harder and better than most other workers. I'd also been studying after hours and on my weeks off to acquire new knowledge and skills. I'd checked out repair and regulation manuals from the library at the quarters and attended classes on the functions of platforms and the operation of oil wells. I knew about "downhole" repairs, the complicated repairs to the pipes (and the valves within them) that extended through the geological layers beneath the bay to the vast oil reservoirs further below. I also learned about the geology of the area and the complications of drilling new wells in East Bay. I worked hard to understand the more advanced technology of oil production because I had a goal in mind: I wanted to be the first female lease operator in East Bay.

Shell always claimed to support employees' advancement through self-study, but in two years, promotions, raises, and recognition were slow in coming my way even though my work evaluations were always outstanding.

Now I was going to be given my first opportunity to "break out" of the work gang and learn a new job. I was going to be trained to maintain the navigational safety equipment at each well or platform—the lights, horns, and other warning equipment required as markers by the Coast Guard, and the solar panels and energy storage systems that supported them. Because these were "Aids to Navigation," the work role was known as "NAVAIDS." I got no raise in pay, and my job title wasn't changed, but I leaped at the opportunity anyway. I was ready for the new challenge and wanted to see the important work of maintaining the navigation safety facilities work done well.

Arley Flowers, a southern Louisiana native with a reputation for laziness, was to train me. As we boarded the thirty-foot jo-boat specially equipped for NAVAIDS I immediately began to familiarize myself with the supplies, the number of pieces of each needed to be kept in stock on the boat, and where they were stowed. I loaded up many carbonaire batteries, which were currently being used to run the lights and horns after dark. (Later, I would help uncover a kickback scheme that led to the wasteful purchase of these non-rechargeable batteries instead of the lead-based rechargeable batteries that could be used with the solar panels at the installations.) As I loaded the boat with supplies, I fully expected that Arley and I would be travelling in it all day from one NAVAIDS facility to another.

I was wrong. Arley took us straight from the quarters to a platform operated by a friend of his called Bat. We went upstairs to visit and never left the platform that day. Arley and Bat spent the day lounging, telling jokes, and relaxing on company time.

I felt restless and bored. I'd always given my employers a full day's work for my pay. Mid-morning and several times later that day, I asked Arley, "Shouldn't we be out in the field doing something?"

"No, today is Thursday," Arley replied with a sly look at Bat. "Nothing is really expected of us. We will do it tomorrow."

"Learn to take it easy," Bat added. "You're not in the gang no more."

They were right about that, I thought to myself. I remembered how the gang pushers had kept us moving from one physically demanding task to another. I liked that. If I had to slow down to Arley's turtle pace, I would get as fat as he was.

In the evening Arley reluctantly took me out to the NAV-AIDS equipment on Bat's platform. He showed me how to change the light bulbs, check the sensor switch that turned the equipment on at nightfall, and test the rotor motor that turned the miniature lighthouse.

At the end of the shift Arley began to fill out the paperwork to account for our time spent during the day. Arley falsified these documents, listing tasks we hadn't performed. This dishonest practice was called "boilerhousing," and I disliked it deeply. Besides, it was grounds for dismissal. Fortunately for me, as a trainee I did not have to affix my signature to the form. Arley seemed to relish boilerhousing, though. In fact, it was the only thing I saw that day that he was really good at.

On the second day of NAVAIDS training, we actually worked! I learned to take cathodic readings that would determine how much the salt water had corroded the underwater supports for the well jackets and platforms. These readings would tell the engineers when divers with scuba equipment and underwater welding torches should be sent to make repairs. I began to hope that my willingness to work and learn was motivating Arley.

By day three, my hopes were rudely dashed. Arley began a revolting campaign of sexual harassment as we traveled alone on the jo-boat between NAVAIDS facilities.

While the term gender-based harassment refers to bigotry in the distribution of work resources and rewards, the term sexual harassment involves sexual touch, display, and threat in the workplace. I'd been sexually harassed on the first night, when Jay had put his arm around me. So from the very first day I'd endured both kinds of discrimination against women in the workplace. Arley's behavior toward me is a pronounced, prolonged example of sexual harassment, though.

He began by making comments about my breasts, my suntan, and my sex life. I told him very firmly that, although I was no prude and enjoyed an off-color joke as much as the next person, I was very happily married and wouldn't think of cheating on my husband.

The situation worsened when, in the late afternoon, I needed to use a restroom. As I've already pointed out, since the day I had been hired my needs as a female for restroom facilities had never been addressed by the company. The men always just urinated overboard, in spite of pollution laws to the contrary, and after I was hired they didn't change their habit at all. Many of the men on work gangs didn't even bother to conceal themselves from me before relieving themselves. I, on the other hand, often endured real pain for as long as twelve hours on work locations without any private spaces. I sure wasn't going to bare my bum for them all to see. I had suffered a severe kidney infection as a child—in fact, I had almost died from it—so holding back was definitely not good for my health. However, when I complained, the bosses told me not to expect special treatment.

My need for a bathroom seemed to provoke Arley into making even more comments. He and I drove to a work barge in the vicinity, where I went down into the bilge with a bucket, as I had done many times before, did my business, and then emptied the bucket over the side, feeling the usual pang of embarrassment. At the next NAVAIDS location, Arley announced that it was his turn. He went to the side of the boat while I sat in the cabin at the wheel.

"Look!" he exclaimed as he returned to the cabin.

Startled, I turned around, only to see him standing there with his penis hanging out of his pants and an ugly smile on his face.

"I've caught my dick in my zipper," he said.

I turned my face away, but not quickly, not wanting him to know that he had embarassed me.

"I'm sure that's happened before. I think you can fix it," I said, sounding as bored and as sarcastic as possible.

"You're a nurse, right? Do you think I should have myself circumcised?"

"I may be a nurse, but that don't mean I'm an urologist. If you have a problem with your dick, go see a doctor. I don't want to look at it."

He had taken his seat beside me by that time, still rolling his penis around in his hand.

I felt very embarassed and humiliated but hid it as well as I could by staring out the front window. Eventually, he put his penis back in his pants and zipped them up. But from that day on, he talked often about his "dick." He complained to me about his wife, telling me that she would not perform oral sex on him and that she would only have sex "doggie" style, as he put it.

Again and again I told him to tell his marital problems to a sex therapist and not to me.

He kept brushing up against my breasts—something I tried to ignore—so he began pulling the neckline of my T-shirts out. I grabbed his hand and yelled "Stop it!" whenever he did, but that never seemed to curtail his advances.

I began to feel as if I were locked on a boat with a pervert.

One afternoon while we were both in the cabin on our way from one location to another, Arley began to masturbate in front of me.

"Damn it, Arley. Put your dick back in your pants. This is just not a normal way for people to act at work." I was really angry. He just kept on with his hurried up-and-down motion, bringing himself to the verge of ejaculation.

I grabbed the paper towels and tossed some at him as I strode for the door. "When you get through with that project, let me know. I'm going out on the deck until it's over."

He was willing to stop now that his audience was walking out. "Oh, all right," he said, as he closed his pants up.

But I didn't turn around and spent the rest of the trip on the deck, mulling over the situation I was in.

I had never been in such a position before. It was strange and new to me. I'd let him know how unwelcome his advances were, how unpleasant I found them, and yet he just kept on touching me without my permission, commenting on my body and his sex life, and exposing himself to me. What was happening here? Was this part of Ervin Floyd's "whatever was necessary" to get me out of East Bay?

My job was hanging in the balance, I thought. This new assignment was my first chance for new experience and responsibility in two years. I couldn't let Arley Flowers drive me away from my chances. And if this was Ervin Floyd's way of getting to me, it just wasn't going to work. I was going to be a better person, a stronger person, than any of them were. They weren't going to drive this woman out!

As I look back on that decision, as well as many others, I think now that I made a mistake. If I could do it over again,

I would force him to turn the boat around and go back to the office, where I would have made a complete report, exposing him for what he was. If I could have lived it over again, I would have reported Nick Claire for calling me a whore on the first day. I was much too tolerant of the sick behavior of some of the men. However, if I'd addressed the problems instantly instead of letting them accumulate, I am sure that I would never have lasted eight-and-a-half years at Shell. I now think, "Act!—and let the chips fall where they may," but then I just wanted to keep my job.

For three weeks I endured Arley's displays and comments in the close quarters of the NAVAIDS jo-boat. I still carry the burden of that experience with me, the feeling of having been soiled, the anger that I was being treated so vulgarly just because I was a woman. I began to hate Arley Flowers.

I was never afraid of him, though. In fact, I'd never been as possessed by those fears as some women are. Not only was I taller and stronger than most women and many of the men on the job, I'd measured my own capacity for violence at an early age. I knew what it felt like to receive and throw blows and was prepared physically and psychologically to grasp the nearest tool to defend myself if anyone threatened harm.

But Arley's behavior embarassed and humiliated me. Did he treat his wife this way? His sister? His mother? What would he do if someone treated his wife the way he was treating me? He was utterly despicable, and yet I felt little faith that anyone in the company would feel as enraged as I felt.

Even by the end of the three-week training period I still had not learned essential tasks, such as installing new solar panels and troubleshooting the warning horns. In week four I was supposed to handle the job on my own with a helper, and the way it looked I was not going to be ready.

"It will be embarassing for both of us if I don't know how to run the job next week, so why don't you teach me about the Class A equipment?" I urged him, hoping to keep his mind on his job.

I studied the regulations and manuals on my own in the meantime and by the fourth week was fairly well prepared, and certainly glad to be free of the pervert I'd been locked up with for what had seemed like an eternity.

I set up a schedule with the new helper to visit all the locations where NAVAIDS facilities were. That meant twenty-four platforms and about 300 oil well satellite structures called well jackets. What we found amazed us. Every site we visited was in need of repair. Arley's lax work habits were putting all night water traffic in jeopardy. My new assistant, Matt, and I worked well together until he was transferred and I had to begin training over again. So many repairs needed to be ordered that I began to do the simple ones myself, just to get them up and working. Besides, the supervisor of the mechanics, Lewis Pastee, began to pressure me about a Coast Guard inspection scheduled for the end of my second month in charge.

"What was going on here?" I asked myself and Lewis. For years the work had been left unattended. Why should I be held accountable for catch-up repairs that should take months?

Nevertheless, I threw myself into the job, working as smart and as hard as I could, and when the Coast Guard inspected the NAVAIDS facilities it gave me a clean report. I was proud of my accomplishment. Not only had I rescued an important facility from neglect, I'd trained two others to continue the work. I had to pat myself on the back alone, though, because no congratulations came down from the supervisors.

And although I was no longer working closely with Arley Flowers, I continued to be the brunt of his sexual perversion. After I was assigned platform duties he would come out on a boat alone just to display himself. I came to look upon his displays with the indifference one looks at an erection on a male animal. He would grab my shirt or brush against my breasts whenever I had to use the boat shop facilities where he'd been reassigned. Once when I was accidentally knocked overboard by a crane, Arley beat everybody else to lift me out of the water. Everyone began to notice how much attention he paid to me. "You can bet that whenever B.J. needs something from the boat shop, Arley will be there to do the job," they would say to one another jokingly. But none of them offered to talk to me about it.

I told no one about Arley's sexual harassment of me, figuring that I would find no supporters among the men of East Bay. The experiences were too deeply humiliating for me to share with just anyone. One evening, though, I decided to give a man of East Bay a chance. While passing the time in casual after-hours conversation with Hank, the night supervisor, I told him how Arley would pull out his penis when there was no one else around. Hank was angry. "That son-of-a-bitch should be shot, but I expected him to be that way. He's always sucking up to the bosses."

Unfortunately, his reaction confirmed my sense that nothing would be done by the company to protect me from Arley Flowers. I would continue to endure the experiences alone.

Solitude became my only defense from the ugly humiliation of gender-based and sexual discrimination. I spent most of my evenings alone, finishing my work day with a session of weight-lifting and jogging around the barrier island before a shower and a meal. Sometimes in the evening I went out to fish by myself or even take the frisbee to play catch alone. Or I would read or watch TV in my room. Movies, card games, ping pong, pool, and ball games were always going on, but I held myself aloof from them. As one of my supervisors observed about me, "B.J. is choosy about her friends." He didn't know that I felt too flayed to open myself up to more harassment after work hours.

As I now understand the impact of these first two years on me, I was building a wall around myself to create a feeling of safety in a very threatening environment. Solitude in itself had never been unpleasant, but isolation in times of trouble feels different. It feels like emptiness.

And as if I had schizophrenia, I felt more and more at odds with myself, less and less like a whole person. For instance, I'd been detaching myself from my own feelings when I sat in my boss's office in order to hear the patronizing, destructive tone of his evaluations without responding to them. What choice did I have? It was "take it or go to the bank." As time wore on I found it harder and harder to put myself back together on my weeks off. The empty wasteland stretched more vastly around me when the abuse by my co-workers began to affect my marriage as well.

Researchers still disagree on the ways biological differences between men and women translate into differences in apti-tudes, thinking, and behavior. But no one disputes the fun-

damental fact that, as far as organs of reproduction and elimination go, men and women are built differently. And so, in justice, men and women require different accommodations for relieving themselves.

Furthermore, custom, if not instinct, leads people to seek privacy when natural biological functions call. Yet when B.J. tried to assert her right to accommodations and to privacy, she was accused of seeking "special treatment."

By denying her claim to these basic human needs, the company representatives put her health at risk. They also played a role in exposing her to what many women would agree is a nightmarish situation.

One of the most terrifying components of sexual assault that a woman can imagine was realized in B.J.'s situation: the absence of an escape route. She was alone in the middle of a vast watery area with no witnesses, no help, and no options. Had the pervert on the boat been physically violent instead of merely narcissistic, B.J.'s well-being would certainly have been in danger.

In refusing to recognize B.J.'s legitimate biological needs the company was not, as it claimed, refusing to give a woman "special treatment." It was, instead, preserving the special treatment it offered men. In justice, the legitimate biological differences of the sexes—and of individuals within each sex— ought to be accommodated when a company hires an individual.

Women should not have to put up with the sexual harassment that is permitted by the lax accommodations provided by employers who set them up with "men only" in mind. Women aren't asking for special treatment; they're asking that the special treatment given men be terminated.

6

SCENES FROM A MARRIAGE

Sexual harassment and discrimination situations are a bit like the old medieval story of St. George the knight, who battled a fierce, fire-breathing dragon while a damsel waited on the sidelines wringing her hands in distress. In the case of gender terrorism, a confrontation is taking place, but the characters are different. St. George is the dragon, and no one—no one— is likely to ride up in gleaming armor to the rescue.

As a woman faces a gender terrorist's dislike or manipulation of her femaleness, she has no alternative but to grab that sword and shining breastplace and wield them on her own behalf. The damsel-in-distress was never very useful as a role model, anyway, since rescuers are so long in coming and so unreliable when they finally get there. Becoming one's own knight-in-shining-armor can, as well, actually make one more complete as a woman in the long run.

Being ostracized, disapproved of, and deserted sets a dreadful challenge for any person. For most people, especially women, our affectionate and love relationships are central to

our sense of personal well-being and comfort. In times of
stress we crave approval and support from co-workers, friends,
and family.

Yet, especially if a woman's difficulty with a boss, teacher,
or co-worker is sexual in nature, a woman's partner may not
come through for her with support. This was true for B.J.

∽ The anger directed at me by the men at East Bay took
both my husband Joe Holcombe and me utterly by surprise.
My work experience at the telephone company and at General
Motors clearly prepared me for the work I was asked to do
there, and I was tough and physically hardy enough for any
traditionally "man's" job. So it simply never occurred to us
that my co-workers might reject me. I worked with men all of
my adult life—in the Air Force, at Michigan Bell, at General
Motors—and I never had that kind of trouble.

Joe clearly supported my decision to take the job, even going
with me to New Orleans for my third set of interviews and
waiting in a coffee shop on the ground floor of One Shell
Square while I interviewed with Will Word, the relieving
superintendent. Afterwards, I and Will Word went down so
that I could introduce Joe. Will asked Joe what he thought
about my taking a job offshore. He told Will, "B.J. has my
full support in anything she does. If she says she can handle
it, I'm quite sure she can."

But both of us were utterly naive, and we suffered for it. At
East Bay I was under attack, in a sense, from the time I walked
onto the work location to the time I left at the end of the week.
Like most people under such enormous pressure, I found it
difficult to adjust my attitude when I returned home to Joe. I

came to feel that he was one of the enemies. Those men at East Bay who harassed me unrelentingly started a chain reaction that destroyed my happy eight-year-long marriage.

I called Joe twice during my first week on the job at East Bay. In tears, I told him that the men hated me just because I was a woman. He wanted me to walk out and come home, but I decided that I would stick out the week and talk it over with him on my first week off. However, as soon as I got home and we began to explore the week's events in detail, Joe became very angry. He was ready to go get the men who had treated me so badly and choke them. I was surprised at his intensity, and unconsciously I began to soften my stories. I wanted to give the job a chance to work out.

After a week of discussion we decided that I would stick with Shell for a while at least, and perhaps give the men some time to adjust and me some time to prove myself. Yet with every week's hitch, more harassment took place, and with every week off my stories of the harassment disturbed Joe more and more.

"Why are you taking this abuse, B.J.?" he began to ask. I didn't exactly have an answer for his question. I simply wanted to tell someone what I had been going through. And I was sure that if I just hung in there, eventually I would establish myself in the men's eyes, and they would stop their harassment.

In the fourth month, however, an event took place that led to a turningpoint in our marriage: a rape attempt by the man who accosted me in the theatre the first night I was there.

After the episode in the theatre my first night at East Bay, I didn't go back to the theatre for a long time, because I wasn't going to put myself in a vulnerable position. I didn't talk to Jay for probably two months, but I was around him sometimes

91

as work required. One day we were in a crew working on a jack-up barge—one that can be jacked up to work like a stationary platform. We were at the boat shop. We were changing gears on the barge, and Jay was also on the location. I was doing something at a vise when Jay came up to me and said, "You're afraid of me, aren't you?"

I looked into his face. His teeth were jagged, something my nurse's training had taught me was a sign that some time in his past he had let a case of syphillis go untreated. I remembered how the health department had come out to the quarters and taken him in for treatment a few weeks before.

"No, I'm not afraid of you," I answered. "But I'll tell you one thing. If you ever put a hand on me again, I'll kill your black ass."

"Well, I don't want you to be afraid of me. I'm really sorry I did that that night in the theatre, and it won't never happen again."

I said, "Well, I appreciate that." But I never said that I believed him.

Two months later he came into my room while I was asleep, intent on raping me. It was about 2:00 A.M., although at the time I didn't know how late it was. The next day was the week's end, and I fell asleep early in order to be rested for my return to land and home. Someone was speaking my name and touching me. I was disoriented, confused—and terrified. It had to be a man, since I was still the only woman at East Bay. That dark shape looming above me was about to force himself on me.

Panic brought me to my senses. I struggled loose of my blankets. Then I kicked at him as hard as I could. My heel connected with some soft part of him, throwing him off balance. He fell. I took my only chance. I scrambled out of the bed and over the dark mass on the floor. Just as he began to lunge back at me, I charged for the door. As I pulled it open, the light from the hallway fell on my attacker. It was Jay, the same man who had promised me that he would never bother me again.

Then the smell hit me: he was drunk. I had no idea where he got the booze from. Liquor was illegal out there—and no firearms, no weapons.

He was still calling my name as I stumbled down the hallway, heading for I didn't know where. When I passed the reading room down the hall, I saw someone in there, someone who would help me, I hoped. I put my hand on his shoulder and spun him around, crying, "There's someone in my room. He's drunk." I looked into the glassy eyes of Dirty Carl. He was drunk, too.

Shoving Carl's bobbing, wobbling bulk back into a chair, I took off for the galley. The cook would be there working on breakfast, and I could get a cup of coffee and sit in a bright place for a while.

"What are you doing up at this hour, B.J.?" he asked as I slipped panting into the kitchen.

I told him what had just happened, and he tried to calm me down.

"Go report it to the Night Clerk. You have to. Go on."

I drank a slow cup of coffee and let the trembling pass as I told him the whole story. Later, I went over to the Night Clerk, who offered to report it to the Production Foreman, the main supervisor of the operation.

But four months of harassment had worn down my morale. I was too hurt, scared, perplexed, and tired. "No, don't report it," I said. "I'm trouble just being here."

The next morning as I returned to the barge for duty as usual, everyone seemed to know about the incident. The Foreman picked me up at 9:00 A.M. "Employee Relations wants to know what you will do if they do not fire the employees involved in the incident last night."

With the morning light, my courage was back. As well as my sense of outrage. They were considering not firing the men! Although I looked him straight in the eye, my voice was trembling. "If something is not done, I will not return to work next week. This is the second time the same man has tried to molest me, and I will not stand for it."

Dirty Carl had all of his gear with him on the noon boat to town as that week's hitch changed; Jay was fired, too, I learned later. They were fired for having liquor at the work location.

When I got home that day I told Joe about it. The fear was still strong inside me, and I anticipated getting some comfort and support from my husband. Instead, I became his victim as well. His volcanic anger, which had been building up for four months, erupted, and it all flowed toward me: "I can't believe that you're taking this awful treatment, B.J.," he raged. "How can you put up with it? You used to be a strong person." We argued for hours heatedly, him treating me the way many partners of rape victims do—by blaming me, the victim. While a rape victim's partner may accuse her of having brought the rape on herself by walking on the wrong street, wearing the wrong clothes, or associating with the wrong people, my husband responded by telling me that I was wrong to stick to the job.

Finally, Joe delivered the ultimatum that had been forming over the past four months: "B.J., you're absolutely stupid to continue. I will not be a part of it any longer. Either you quit that job right now, or I don't ever want to hear another word about it." With that, he walked out. He was closing the door, was refusing to be my confidant and support. From then on I was to be utterly alone in my trouble.

So began the rift that was to widen so painfully between my husband and me.

The closing of the door between us was especially painful because we had always been so open, so communicative with one another. In fact, I was blessed with the kind of marriage most women only get to fantasize about. We were introduced by a mutual friend while we were both at Shepard Air Force Base in Texas. I was in Air Force medical training, and Joe, having already been to Vietnam and Korea, was in an advanced school for jet aircraft mechanics. This was in the fall of 1971. Our closeness sprang up as suddenly as surprise lilies and brought us both breathtaking delight.

We began to spend all our free time together. We danced at the NCO club, saw movies, drank Texas Red Draw—beer and tomato juice—and all the while we talked. Our conversations sometimes lasted all day and all night. Within three months we knew that our emotions and thoughts had become so intertwined that we wanted to stay together. Unfortunately, the military service is not always kind to romance.

Joe was sent to Homestead Air Force Base in south Florida, while I had to stay at Shepard, Texas. To say goodbye to him hurt me, as if something had been ripped out from under my skin. We did our best to stay connected, writing letters and love poems, mailing photographs and, of course, talking on the phone. Once I was able to get leave to visit him, and we spent three delirious days and nights together. Finally, I was assigned to Eglin Air Force Base in the Florida panhandle, a twelve-hour car drive but only a two-hour plane ride from Homestead. Also, the military telephone network was available to us after hours. We took full advantage of our now-more-manageable distance. Still, it was excruciating to have access to the personality but not the presence of the man I loved.

During one of our all-night telephone calls, Joe asked me to marry him. I was thrilled and accepted with all my heart, but I wouldn't agree to be married right away. After all, in early 1972 the shadow of death in Vietnam loomed large for military personnel, especially for fliers in the Air Force. While I wanted to be with him, I felt that if he were sent to southeast Asia I would need the support and distraction of my job at Eglin to sustain me in the inevitable anxiety. For weeks our phone conversations concerned only my reluctance to marry a man who might suddenly be taken from me. One night a voice broke into our debate on the phone line, which was not a private line. "Marry him, lady," was what the voice said.

Well, eventually I did. Joe told me it was now or else, and I agreed. He flew up to Eglin, and we were married on March 25, 1972, by a Justice of the Peace at the quaint county court-house in the small Florida panhandle town of Crestview. As we departed hand-in-hand from the old two-story building and walked under the oaks that lined the sidewalk, I saw the Spanish moss wafting in the warm spring breeze. I wondered what the future would waft our way.

What happened fulfilled both our hopes and our fears. Within two months I had succeeded in getting transferred to Homestead Air Force Base, and within a month of my settling in there Joe got ordered to Vietnam. The cruelty of fate undermined my strength, and I spent hours in tears. Newly situated in Homestead, I had no friends to sustain me as I feared for Joe's wellbeing in that horrifying theatre of war. I wrote long letters and worked twelve to sixteen hours a day, trying to exhaust myself. Nevertheless, I slept very little and instead found myself taking long late-night car drives into the Everglades, the Sea of Grass, where the desolation matched my mood.

Four months later the troop withdrawal began, and Joe, I thanked heaven, was sent home. Our reunion was thrilling. He was astonished to see me twenty-five pounds lighter; I felt that I never wanted to let him go. Our closeness was renewed, and we made a vow never to let anything separate us again. We both sought and were granted honorable discharges from the Air Force, and we moved to Michigan, where I expected to be trained as a Physician's Assistant and he was finally hired as an aircraft mechanic as a member of the Air National Guard.

From Michigan to Florida we kept that vow to stay together. In remodeling a house and reselling it for a profit, we showed what we could accomplish as a team. We had both earned college degrees and felt that our next step was financial security. The move to the Pensacola area had brought career obstacles, but until this rupture we had lived under each other's skin. Now we were growing more and more separate.

While I was determined to defy the men who were trying to drive me out of my high-paying, challenging oil-production job, Joe wanted me to cave in. He began to express resentment as I drove off with my carpool at the beginning of each week-long hitch. Carpooling was a standard practice for East Bay employees from all over the Gulf Coast region—Alabama, Mississippi, Louisiana, and Florida—who would meet at mutually agreeable spots and carpool to the boat terminal south of New Orleans, splitting traveling expenses. I drove with Matt and Lee, two Shell Oil employees who lived in Opp, a small town in Alabama just north of Pensacola. They would drive down to Pensacola by 2:00 A.M., and we would all climb into my Colt, the most economical of our cars, and be boarding the boat for East Bay by 8:00 A.M. I would usually drive the first half of the trip, then Matt would take over. We never let Lee drive, because he was usually drunk. Besides, his driver's license had been suspended for driving under the influence.

Joe objected that no husband in his right mind would allow his wife to drive off with two other men in the middle of the night. This jealousy was obviously trumped up; he knew there was nothing going on between Matt, Lee, and me. But he was using every device he could come up with to make me feel guilty.

Still, with every new experience of harassment that I had to bear alone, I became more and more resentful of him. I knew, for instance, that if he had been willing to listen to the story about the Peeping Tom who had been looking through the door grill at me as I got out of the shower, he would have been very jealous and angry indeed. I bitterly kept that news from Joe.

The news was kept from me for quite a while, too. I found

out about this Peeping Tom by accident, actually. Matt had borrowed my car to go back to New Orleans a day before the week's end, so I had to hitch a ride from the terminal to the city. At first I asked a warehouseman, a steady worker and a religious man whom I repected. He was African-American. Generously, he said he would be glad to give me a lift. Within a day, though, the rumor mill was grinding: I was a "Nigger Lover" because "out of all the decent men who worked there, I had asked a 'Nigger' for a lift." One of the men I worked with made sure I knew what was being said. I was deeply embarassed about the uproar. I apologized to the warehouseman for causing him the humiliation and told him I would find a ride with someone else.

The next person I asked was Freddie, a white man I got along well with. I was criticized for this choice later, too. Although Freddie had always been pleasant to me, his alcoholism meant that I'd gone from bad to worse. Again, someone came up and told me this rumor. All this brouhaha simply because I needed a ride that would last no more than an hour and a half! In exasperation, I stuck with my second choice and ignored what others said.

Ultimately, as a result of this ride I was the dubious beneficiary of the gossip network. While we rolled down the road, me driving while Freddie drank the vodka he had bought at a roadside store, we talked about projects at work. Finally he said, "I know that you know someone lies out in the reading room and watches you come out of the shower every day."

"No, I didn't know that," I replied, trying to hide my surprise from this man I didn't know very well. "Who is it? How does he do it?"

"Well, he just lies on one of the sofas in the reading room and looks through the grill at the bottom of the door. He says you have a big bush."

A shock of shame and anger flashed through me like lightning. My face felt hot, and my pulse was throbbing in my neck. How dare he! Gripping the steering wheel until my knuckles were white, I did my best to hide what I felt as Freddie talked on about the man who violated my privacy.

The reading room was at the end of the twenty-foot hallway down the center of the women's quarters. Off-hours employees entered the reading room from an outside door. Often, several people would be enjoying the magazines and newspapers available there when I walked through it at the end of my shift to go into my quarters and shower. I never paid much attention to who was there. I would walk through the doorway into the hallway down the length of the building. At the end opposite the reading room was the shower room, and just beside it along one side was the door to my room. Since I was the only one living in that building, I never even thought to put a bathrobe or towel around me as I stepped from the bathroom into my room; I felt that I was alone in my own house.

I was outraged that I would be spied on when I believed that I was in private, and I was even more outraged when Freddie told me that the snoop was the son-in-law of one of the supervisors. Did this supervisor's daughter, the Peeping Tom's wife, know her husband was playing the voyeur? Did the supervisor know and keep her husband's behavior secret from his daughter? How many other workers besides Freddie, who had never told me, knew about this?

Did Nancy, who worked the weeks I was off and slept in the other bunk in the same room, know what was happening?

Was the same man peering at her, too? We usually exchanged information when we saw one another as shifts changed. I decided to ask her about it when I saw her the following Thursday and find out what she'd heard about it.

For the remainder of the drive, Freddie sipped his vodka and spilled more beans. By the time we got to New Orleans and found Matt waiting with my car at the prearranged spot, I was deeply disturbed. I drove the entire way home as an excuse to keep myself occupied so I could think.

That week I resented Joe intensely for being unwilling to listen. I was isolated. My resentment deepened as I mowed the lawn, which he hadn't mowed, saw after the tenants of our apartment building, whom he had ignored, and prepared meals for him for the upcoming week, all in response to the guilt he made me feel about "deserting" him.

By the time I returned to East Bay the next week, I was loaded for bear. I confronted Nancy with the rumor of the man looking through the hall door grill, and she admitted that she'd heard of it. "I just thought it was harmless," she said. "I tape a big piece of cardboard over the grill myself, but it always gets torn off."

"Well, I intend to do something about it," I vowed.

When I went to the shower that evening, I took a large bath towel with me. I turned the hallway light off as I went in. After my shower, I wrapped myself in the towel, turned off the bathroom light, and crept down the hall as quietly as I could. I snatched open the reading room door and, sure enough, there lay the culprit stretched out on the green sofa with his face toward the grill in the door.

"What the hell do you think you are doing?" I said as sternly as I could muster. "Somebody should paddle your rear, or take you by the ear and tell your wife on you." Others in the reading room looked up from their magazines and newspapers, grinning at his embarassment.

He was beet red, even on the tops of his ears. "I don't know what you're talking about," he stammered.

"You don't, huh? Somebody told me about how you come here to watch me come out of the shower every day after my shift. He told me that you're spreading stories about my body. You're some kind of sick person, in my opinion, and I think we should go to the boss."

As I was hurling my accusations, he was scrambling off the green sofa and backing out of the reading room. "Woman, you are crazy," he called over his shoulder as he made his retreat.

Later that evening I taped a big piece of cardboard over the grill in the door, just as Nancy had done. By the next day, the cardboard was nowhere to be found. I tried again, but again the cardboard disappeared. In disgust, I reported it to the Production Foreman, who was in charge of the maintenance of the living quarters. He tried several different ways of blocking the view through the wide vents and finally installed two grills with the vents positioned in opposite directions so that there would be no way to peer through them. This blocked the Peeping Tom's peephole, but the episode left me feeling very much alone. The rumor mill ground away around me; I was the subject of much discussion—lies, to be more precise— with no friends to defend me. And I'd been abandoned by my husband, who had been, but no longer was, my best friend.

When I would return to Pensacola after my week at work, we would take the dog for a walk in the lovely bayside park near our home. We would be very glad to see one another.

But within an hour or two, arguments would start. We would fight over the messy house, the unmowed lawn, the oil spotting the driveway, or the numerous errands left undone. Our fights about petty domestic details got nasty. Why should I spend my week off cleaning up after him when I was enduring hell on our behalf and not even getting to talk about it?

Soon we were no longer really arguing about housekeeping but instead were locked in a power struggle. That was clearly behind our argument about the pile of decorative rocks that Joe had purchased for a landscaping project and never used. After having to move them for the third time in order to mow the lawn, I got fed up beyond endurance and barked at him, "Get your ass out there and move those rocks!" I used the same tone of voice that I used with the men in the work gang. I saw immediately from the set of his jaw that those rocks would stay there until the land washed into the sea. From that point on Joe did less and less around the house, and as a consequence I spent my week off doing more and more.

Our arguments also concerned money, which I'd always managed because I was good at it and Joe wasn't. In fact, he let money slip through his fingers and had nothing to show for it. We'd struggled through lean periods as students, eating on fifteen or twenty dollars a week for a while, but our attitude was always "Ain't we got fun!" Now that my salary was costing me so much in pain and loneliness, I became more aware of every penny. My mistrust of Joe's spending habits grew as he made thoughtless purchases during the weeks I was away. He was a credit card junkie.

What I didn't know at the time was that Joe was becoming a Valium junkie as well. His job dissatisfaction and our arguments aggravated his ulcers as well as the stuttering that had plagued him since his first hitch in Vietnam, when he watched a buddy die right beside him from shrapnel caught in his jugular vein. Joe made an appointment with our family physician, studied my old Physician's Desk Reference from my nursing days, and invented the appropriate symptoms. He then told the doctor that he was upset because his wife threatened to commit suicide and suggested that the doctor give him a prescription for Valium. The doctor asked no questions.

Joe began abusing the mood-altering drug, daydreaming about sailing to Tahiti and studying books about sailing. To make him more tranquil, he would take three pills just before I returned from my week at work. Besides taking Valium like candy, he was drinking alcohol, too—a deadly combination. I hated him to be drugged up. He was like a zombie.

We did buy a sailboat, which soon became just something else to fight about. When something went wrong while we were out on the water, we blamed one another. When he bought something for the boat, we argued about money. He was like a tyrant on the boat. He was its captain, and everyone on the boat had to do what he said. Soon, neither I nor any family and friends would go out on it with him, so the boat stayed in the marina a lot. That depressed him even more than the drugs.

About a year and a half of conflict finally drove him to see a clinical psychologist. Everything had bottled up inside him, because he didn't confide in anyone about our problems any more than I did. He unloaded on the psychologist and told her everything he thought about his lousy life.

The psychologist soon led Joe to think about divorce, and so I came to look upon her as an enemy, too. Joe's story was that he was talking and happened to say, "I would sure hate to get a divorce," and the psychologist replied—and these were her exact words, according to Joe—"Well, it's not the end of the world." I was outraged at the psychologist for trying to break up our marriage. I went in to talk with her. I told her that she didn't know anything about Joe and me and to keep her nose out of my life. The next time Joe saw the psychologist she advised him that our marriage should probably be ended. When Joe first said that he wanted a divorce, something died in my soul. This was the man I loved and wanted to be with.

I was able to convince him to drop the psychologist who had advised the divorce and to try again. I agreed to see a therapist because I wanted to start over. He secretly kept spending money on Valium, and I was still not confiding in him about my problems on the job. Two months later, in the middle of yet another argument, Joe asked for a divorce again. By this time, I had had it: "Okay, you son of a bitch, I'll give you a divorce." I arranged the paperwork, and then he conscientiously went down to the sheriff's department to pick up the papers in order to avoid being charged the fee for delivering the summons. Even then, we were obviously still cooperating for our mutual benefit.

Although the divorce was final in December of 1982—it took only two years for Shell Oil to wreck our marriage—we kept living in our home together while we were waiting for it to sell. Our divorce didn't change our bickering or Joe's drug use. He retreated into an enormous self-centeredness, and I was bitter and withdrawn.

When the house finally sold in March of 1983, we liquidated our other resources and split the money. When he left me, Joe had many thousands of dollars in his pocket. Within six months he'd spent it.

I rented an old farmhouse and became a recluse, determined to make promotions on my job my purpose in life. I was no longer seeing a therapist because I'd discovered that my employee benefits didn't cover the costs of psychological counseling. Neither did I talk any more with my sister, who next to Joe had been my closest friend. In fact, she'd been more like a daughter than a sister because my mother brought her home from the hospital when I was fifteen and handed her to me. "Here, she's yours," Ma said. But I'd lost confidence in her, too, when she, like Joe, began to question my motives for sticking with my job. As a consequence, I had no one to trust and confide in. I've never found it easy to ask for help, and especially not then, when my primary friends were accusing me of the worst motives in keeping my job. My mistrust of people and my self-isolation became a habit.

Joe moved in with a friend, Brad. He still showed up on my doorstep when I was home from work, and I always let him in. Secretly, I was glad to see him, but I didn't let myself show it. And I didn't do his housework anymore.

I began to suffer illnesses. Just a few months after we got separate residences, I ended up in the hospital with septicemia, an internal infection. He sent flowers but never came by to see me while I was there. After I got back to my house, he came to tell me that he was on his way to his first date with a woman from work that he had been attracted to. I was astonished. "Why did you come by to tell me that?" I tried to portray an attitude of indifference—he'd wanted to be divorced from me, and so be it—but I really didn't feel that way. I was torn up inside. For my part, I mistrusted men, and the last thing I wanted was to see anyone else.

Not that I didn't have my chances. In fact, the pusher of the gang I had been working on had fallen in love with me, although I didn't realize it.

I'd always been very grateful for Maurice, because he was one gang pusher who treated me fairly. As an example, one of my co-workers on the gang, Wayne "Squint" Nightbird, had always resisted my authority. Not only did I have seniority over Wayne, I was lead roustabout, and my orders were supposed to be followed. One day we were unloading pipes from our barge to a platform called "Knockout #2." Since the pipes were too heavy and bulky for lifting and carrying by hand, the work crews always used the cranes situated on the barge and on the platforms. Maurice told me to go up to the top of the platform and run the crane to lift the supplies off the barge.

By the time I ran up the eighty steps to the first floor and then the two flights to the top level where the crane was, Wayne was already sitting there.

I said, "Wayne, get off the crane."

"No, I won't, B.J. I want to pick up those supplies off the barge. You go hook up for me."

"Wayne, Maurice sent me up here to do that. You'd better get off the crane."

"Ain't no woman telling me what to do," he sassed back.

So I went down and got back onto the barge. I began giving him the hand signals that told him how far to let out the crane's line, so that I could hook the line onto the wires around the first sheaf of pipes. As I began attaching the lines to the pipe sheaves, Maurice walked out of the barge's cabin.

"What the hell are you doing out here? I told you to get up there and run that crane."

"Maurice," I protested, "I went up there. Wayne wouldn't get off the crane, and there ain't nothin' I can do about it. I'm not fighting him."

Then his eyes squinted up. "I'll handle that right now. Don't hook up another thing." And he strode off toward the stairway with his hands made into fists.

As he stomped up those three flights of metal grate stairs, the platform reverberated with the scolding Maurice was planning. He went up to the top deck and got Squint down.

"Don't you ever, and I mean *ever*, tell B.J. that you're not doing what she says. If I'm not here and she's in charge, or even if I am here and I give her an order that she gives you, you'd better follow it."

Of course, that didn't stop Wayne. If Maurice wasn't around, he would still defy my orders with a snide smile. Wayne knew that I wouldn't tell Maurice, because that would be like a child "snitching" on another child. It would be a violation of a code that says that a "man" handles "his" own problems.

But Maurice was the only boss in my eight years at Shell who got mad when he saw other men refusing to cooperate with me.

I had earned Maurice's support the honest way, through a year's hard work on his gang. The very first day I was assigned to his gang, though, it seemed that we might have difficulty working together. His Cajun accent was so different from my Appalachian accent that Michael, another member of the gang, had to translate for us. When Michael wasn't around, Maurice would give up trying to tell me what to do and just begin the work himself. Finally, I got impatient. He was hammering on a hammer wrench with a sledge hammer to break loose a rusted bolt. I came up behind him, and when he swung back the sledge hammer for the next blow, I grabbed it.

"I don't know how you feel about this," I said to him, "but you're taking my job. Give me that sledge hammer." From that day on, he didn't do any of my work.

Maurice and I became friends and enjoyed kidding around with one another. At least, those were my feelings. When he told me that he had fallen in love with me, it scared me to death.

He kept it to himself for a long time. One day after being on his gang for more than a year, I walked into the cabin on the boat by the back-up barge where we were working. Maurice was cooking lunch. As I walked in, he grabbed me real tight and kissed me right on the mouth.

I pushed him away. "Why are you doing this, Maurice?" I was actually afraid of him at that moment, even though Maurice had always been kind and respectful to me.

"I'm scared to tell you this, B.J." he said, "but I really do love you."

I turned around and ran right back out of that cabin.

Later that day I went to him and asked him, "Look, Maurice, we've been good friends. What have I ever done to make you feel this way?"

He was honest and straightforward, just as he had been during the year we became friends. "B.J., you haven't done anything, and you haven't said anything wrong. It's my fault. I had to tell you. I would leave my wife and go live with you in the hills of Kentucky if you wanted me to."

Well, I believed him. "You're nuts, you crazy Cajun," I exclaimed. "You had better get this out of your head right now."

"I can't, B.J. I'm with you every day. You're the best worker I've ever had, and besides, you're beautiful. I've got to go to the boss and get a transfer."

I hated to hear him say that. Maurice was well respected by the gang members and would get tranferred off that specific barge, which he really liked. I told him to transfer me instead.

He wouldn't do it. "It's not your fault, B.J., it's mine. You shouldn't have to suffer for it." And within two weeks he was transferred. I fended off many advances offered by men at East Bay, but I knew the difference between their selfishness and Maurice's sincerity.

Besides, from the very first I had always made it clear that I was a married woman, not one looking for a man. Although Joe and I had just divorced at the time of Maurice's declaration of love, I knew that I still loved Joe and didn't want anyone else. Joe kept aggravating my feelings of jealousy, though, and, weakened by loss and conflict, I was manipulated by him.

Joe had a very distinctive pickup truck with a front license plate that said "If guns are outlawed, only outlaws will have guns." Once friends who lived in an apartment complex came to me and asked, "What was Joe's truck doing over in our parking lot all night last Tuesday night?" I said I didn't know. Then I asked him. He went crazy. First he accused me of having had a detective follow him. I laughed at that. I didn't need a detective to know what he was doing; I knew him too well. I felt so torn up inside, though. The next time he left, I was sure he was on his way to a date. I went berserk and threw a metal garbage can at his truck as he pulled away.

One night when we arranged to go out to dinner together, he called and cancelled, telling me that he had to do laundry. I went to his place, which was a mess. His dirty clothes were still there, but he was nowhere to be found. I waited until about 9:00 or 10:00 o'clock, washing dishes and cleaning up, and then went home. I stayed up all night, calling his number at regular intervals. He never came home that night.

The next morning he called me from Sears. He was getting a new set of tires on his truck—using the Sears credit card because he was making no money at the time. I asked him where he was that last night. He said, "I was at my place."

"Joe, why are you lying to me? You weren't there. I was, and if you'd been there, you would know that I was there, because I cleaned up."

"Oh, well, I'm lying to you. I was at Brad's house."

Sure, he was at Brad's house.

Facing the men's dislike at East Bay and my husband's deceit at home was too much for me. I began drinking heavily. My weeks off would evaporate in an alcoholic haze. I would stumble out of bed in the middle of the night and wander off to a bar to trade sad tales with other barflies. By this time I'd moved into another house on a street called Foulis. It was the foul point of my life.

Joe had moved, too. He'd bought some property in the woods in a state forest, and I helped him build a cabin there. He resigned his job entirely, left the house he'd been sharing with Brad, and moved out into that solitary place. He often spent my weeks off with me at Foulis Street, but during my weeks at East Bay he lived by himself in that woodsy isolation.

Within a few months Joe became increasingly obsessed with the threat of nuclear holocaust. He talked constantly about the need for fallout shelters and survival strategies. He even bought us a pair of Israeli-made gas masks as an anniversary gift. Once after he had been out there alone for three weeks, he pointed out very seriously to me that if a murder was committed while he was staying out there, he would lack an alibi if he was accused of it. His friends told me that they feared he was going crazy.

Clearly, we had both arrived at "the dark night of the soul."

Women's experience in the workplace should not be so terrible that their relations with their partners are jeopardized.

B.J.'s experiences at East Bay colored her attitude toward more than just her co-workers. Mistrust and anger toward them leaked into her interactions with her husband. While he felt powerless to protect her from insults and attacks taking place so far away, he also felt powerless to control her decision to continue working. When their communication broke down, the consequences were painful for both of them.

As a woman enduring sexual harassment and discrimination struggles to maintain both her job and her mental balance, she may need extraordinary support and understanding from her partner, her family, and her friends. Eventually, they, too, will begin to feel the stresses and tensions that have their source in the workplace.

The intimate atmosphere of the home often does absorb the stresses and tensions generated in the workplace. It becomes the sponge that mops up many of society's messes.

In that way, an injustice in the workplace poisons more than a single working relationship; the poison can work its way through a whole community.

7

OTHER WOMEN COME TO EAST BAY

❧

Women workers at East Bay, and B.J. particularly, had been thrust into a work environment unprepared to accept them. Some male co-workers were hostile, even life-threatening. This hostility could easily have been predicted and compensated for.

Unfortunately, Shell Oil Company displayed no such foresight. The company's human resources personnel merely implemented equal employment opportunity principles mechanically. But the women hired to work at East Bay were not just statistics in a hiring trend. Instead, they were human beings thrust into a human community. Ironically, Shell's human resources personnel failed to conceive of the women as human resources in a human situation.

For about two years I struggled alone to prove that East Bay was not just a man's world. I was sure that, if I buckled under the pressure and quit my job to escape from the sordid, petty, and humiliating treatment by my co-workers and supervisors, they would use my resignation as an excuse never to hire another woman.

"I'll prove to them that a woman can do this work," I said to myself over and over again. Just as a mantra helps in meditation, that sentence kept me going when my spirits wore down. I looked forward to the day when Shell Oil would hire another woman to work in the labor gang along with me. I knew that she would have to be strong-willed, but having an ally would make things easier for both of us. I never really expected to be the agent for fulfilling my own dreams of a woman co-worker, but I was. And the referral came from the unlikeliest source: my beauty parlor.

My weeks off work always began with a trip to my hairdresser. She never failed to grumble about the dent that circled my hair, made by the inner band of the hard hat I wore all day long during my week offshore. That led to talk about my job, of course, and, like many hairdressers, she was curious. I answered her questions about the pay and other benefits, keeping the ugly details about harassment secret. During one conversation she asked so many questions about the application process that I began to chuckle. She was slim and fashionably dressed, wore high heels, and had dainty hands. She didn't strike me as a very hardy person.

"I don't think you would really want to do work like that. You probably wouldn't like the problems it causes, either."

"Oh, no, I'm not going out on oil platforms." She laughed outright at the thought herself. "But my stepdaughter still lives with me because she can't find work that pays well enough for her to move out. We would both like her to have her own place. Right now she's making minimum wage at a jewelry store."

"Well," I said, ruefully, "she would need to be strong, not just physically but emotionally."

"She is," said her mother with some pride. "She's a big girl and tough, too. You think about it, and if you could help, let me know."

I did think about it, and next week when I went in for my perm, I arranged to meet Valerie and size her up. I decided to tell her about the attitude of my male co-workers toward women laborers at East Bay and let her decide if she wanted to take on the challenge.

Once we met and talked, Valerie's enthusiasm about the opportunity infected me as well. We both agreed that she would have to learn her own ways of coping with the undesirable work conditions, just as I had. She was above average height and weight for a woman—five feet seven inches and 160 pounds. She was blond, nice-looking and, most important, seemed to have a resilient, optimistic personality.

I placed a call to my supervisor, Hoss, who agreed to take her on as a "contract" hand on the next shift. I was elated. Finally, I would have somebody to confide in. I called her at home right away. We would be leaving that night at 2:00 A.M. for the long drive to the terminal south of New Orleans. She would join my carpool and bump in some money to pay for the gas. I told her to pack some old jeans and shirts that she could leave at the company laundry and sent her off right away to buy a pair of steel-toed work boots.

When she joined me and Matt, my other rider, in the wee

hours, she was wide-eyed and giddy with excitment. I remembered very well my similar sensations two years before.

"Did you notify the jewelry store that you won't be there?" I asked.

"Yeah," she answered with a grin and a twinkle in her eye, "but they told me I was crazy and said to be careful." She and Matt hit it off, and her cheerful, talkative manner made the long night drive go by quickly.

We stopped at the contractor's office on the way to the boat terminal from New Orleans. Everything was arranged. Valerie was given a time book and a life jacket and told that her check would be waiting for her at the end of the week. On down the road to the boat terminal, I could see the fatigue in her face in the dawn's soft light. Once on the boat that would take us to the offshore quarters, she drifted off to sleep, just like all the other old hands on board.

We arrived at East Bay, and I took her to the office and introduced her to the supervisors. They shook hands genially enough. Then I showed her to the living quarters, where we met Nancy, the office worker who worked on the opposite crew and lived in my room during the week I was off. Nancy and I usually got a chance to commiserate with one another for a half hour or so as work crews changed off every week.

I saw envy cross Nancy's face as I introduced Val as my new woman co-worker. She was still the solo woman on Crew A. "Well, maybe the next woman to be hired will be assigned to my crew," she sighed. Nancy left to catch the boat back to shore while Val set her things up in the room across the hall from mine, and then we went to the galley for lunch. I would show her the ropes, teach her everything I knew. I wanted this job to work out for her, for my sake as well as for hers.

116

Val's first job assignment was the WSB1, the work barge where I had started out. When I introduced her to the gang of the WSB1, I was agreeably surprised at their friendly, receptive attitude—such a contrast from their coldness to me when I first joined. It was a revelation. I began to think that maybe I'd really made some progress in getting women accepted as oil production laborers. With that hopeful thought in mind, I left Val to make her way through her first day as best she could.

Back at my own work assignment, I fielded a thousand questions from my co-workers about the new woman. They wanted to know all about her.

"She'll never be the worker you are, B.J.," they said.

"Give her a chance. She'll fit in and learn the work," was my reply.

And I was determined that she would.

After the work day was complete, I took Val back to the barge for some after-hours coaching. I showed her all the different pipe fittings and explained the welding equipment. I described the kinds of work she would be expected to do. She was tired but still excited. "This is like camping out to me," she said.

The first week went by smoothly. Val seemed to be happy with the opportunity to learn this new, exciting kind of work. Relationships with her co-workers seemed to be going well.

One problem nagged at me, though. Some of the men's questions about her were very personal: Is she married? Did she have a steady guy? Would she go out with me? I felt strongly that sex and work don't mix, especially offshore. Although rumors that I was sleeping with one man or another were always current, I'd ignored them and felt nothing but scorn for the people who circulated them. I'd been friendly, but that was it. I was married, and even if I wasn't, I certainly wouldn't look for that kind of companionship from my fellow workers. I hoped that the presence of another woman would somehow put a stop to the rumors, but now I realized they would just multiply by two. I began to hold my breath, waiting for the inevitable problems with the men to appear.

My reservations evaporated, at least temporarily, when I saw the pleasure on Val's face as she picked up her check at the end of her first week's shift. $550.00! She'd never made that much money before at one time in her life. Her checks from the jewelry store were $80.00. A woman had just busted out of the minimum-wage ghetto, and, I was proud to say, I'd helped her.

Two hitches later, Val and I were astonished to discover that another woman, Jenny, had been hired by the company to work on our crew and that she would be out on the late boat. She would bunk in Val's room, since the other rooms in what was now being called "the women's quarters" were still being used to store manuals and records. Jenny was five feet five inches tall and a stout 160 pounds. She was attractive, with long dark hair, slim hips, and a large chest. I saw that she caught men's eyes. She was assigned to work in central facilities, which maintained the buildings and equipment on the island, and treated, measured, and shipped the gas and oil that came in from the platforms. I'd originally been hired to do this job, but the production foreman refused to accept me. He'd gone to the field boss, I found out later, and arranged to trade me "for the worst hand the field boss had." I wondered what Jenny would have to put up with on that assignment.

With two female co-workers as companions and confidantes,

my weeks offshore soon became much more enjoyable. Val, Jenny, and I spent our free time after the twelve-hour work days participating in group sports like softball, volleyball, and fishing. These activities had always been available to me, but as the only woman I'd been reluctant to join in and went running by myself instead. Now I enjoyed pool and ping pong—Jenny and I became an unbeatable ping pong team— and I even went back to the theatre to enjoy movies for the first time since Day One.

My life was also safer than it had been before other women came to East Bay. For example, when a man intruded into the building and my bedroom while I was asleep, just as Jay and Dirty Carl had a year earlier, I had help at first hand. Jenny and Valerie had been at East Bay about four years when the second intrusion took place.

I'd fallen asleep while watching a movie on TV. Suddenly I jerked awake to see in the TV's bluish light a large penis and red pubic hair dangling just inches in front of my eyes. It was Harley, otherwise known as Padre, a gangpusher whom I had liked and trusted. Up until now, that is. He was standing right beside my bed with his pants and underwear around his knees and his face screwed up as if he were in some kind of pain.

"Harley, what the hell are you doing in here?" I yelled as loudly as I could.

"Just touch me, B.J.," he whined pathetically. "Please, just touch me."

The fool looked so ridiculous that, in spite of myself, I exploded in laughter. Ordinarily, he was quite a gentleman. Also, he'd told me that his very jealous wife would leave him without a penny to his name if he ever strayed. A midnight visit was the last thing I'd ever expected from Padre.

Guffawing all the while, I leaped from the bed, grabbed some cutoffs from the floor and dashed across the hall to Jenny's room.

"Jenny, you won't frigging believe this! Harley is in my room with his pants down, wanting me to touch him." I was clamoring loudly enough to rouse the whole facility.

Jenny tumbled out of her bunk as I burst in. "You're kidding!"

"No, go look for yourself!"

Jenny burst into laughter as we peered through her door at a red-faced Harley, who had pulled his pants back up and was shamefacedly tiptoeing barefooted from my room. We were still giggling as he picked up his shoes from where he had left them by the door to the building and crept out.

Jenny and I laughed about Harley for some time before returning to bed for sleep. The next day we learned that Valerie, whose room was next to mine, had heard it all as well. I was very glad they were there. Even when I first woke up, I didn't feel the same terror as I had when Jay came into my room before. Then I was the only person in the whole building; now I had two other people available right next door. Feeling so much safer, I could afford a sense of humor; having 250 pounds of sweat and muscle standing over me with his penis hanging out could strike me as funny.

Not all aspects of life at East Bay worked out so well for the other women, though. Several variables combined to create problems for both Val and Jenny. First, neither one of them was physically hardy. Second, neither one of them had any training or background in industrial manual labor before being hired. Third, they let sex overlap with work.

Val was a willing worker on the work gang for the first three months, but in the fourth, when she moved from being a contract worker to an official employee of Shell Oil, she stopped trying as hard, as if she now had it made. Perhaps by that time the novelty of the paycheck had begun to wear off, and she was forced to face the rigors of an outdoor job in the Gulf of Mexico.

The job was very demanding physically, and yet Val gained weight very quickly. Within the first nine months, Val's weight went from 160 pounds, already too much for her five-foot, seven-inch frame, to more than 200 pounds. After all, the meals at the galley were all-you-could-eat, and Valerie wasn't the only person to take more advantage of the buffet than was good for her. But Valerie, like many women, had less upper-body strength than the job often demanded, and the extra weight reduced her endurance and flexibility as well.

One day when a crew was working in the marsh, Val got stuck in the mud and couldn't pull herself out. A crane on the barge had to lift her out. Boarding boats or barges from platforms was also hard for Valerie once she gained extra weight. The maneuver often required swinging over on a rope. The boat might be pitching up and down in rough waters, so the timing of the take-off was important. The gang pushers who supervised Valerie began to complain that she was a safety hazard and shifted her from one kind of job to another, trying to find work she could do. Valerie herself was more and more discontent working in the gang and complained about the heat and the cold.

One morning I saw the gang pusher leave her standing on the dock while he pulled away with the rest of the gang in the barge. He said he would rather work one hand short than have her in the work gang, and he sent her back to the office to get some other work assignment for the day. She and this particular gang pusher had been having conflicts because he gave her bad work evaluations. I'd asked her, "Do you think you deserve better work evaluations?"

"Yeah, I do what everyone else does, but everyone comes along and takes tools out of my hands. They don't want me to do some of the tasks. They want me to clean the tools and clean the barge and help oil and work on the barge all the time."

"Well, if that's what your boss tells you to do, that's what you're supposed to do. He can have you doing anything he needs you to do. But, being a roustabout with nearly a year on the job, you should be able to walk onto any well jacket out there and shut it down all by yourself, knowing what needs to be done and how to do it. You should just go get your tools and start unscrewing the valves and flanges."

I'd groped to familiarize myself with the tools and manual skills, but deduction and observation worked well to help me. For instance, one day in my third hitch I was working on an oil jacket with Rob Smith. He told me to hand him a twenty-four-inch Stillson. I didn't know what a Stillson was. I walked over to the tool case, feeling very dumb. Then I saw a pipe wrench with "Stillson" written right on it. "Stillson" is the company that made it. I thought, "That's what he wants?"

As I was still standing there, he called over to me, "They're hanging right on the side there."

When someone told me to bring him a hammer wrench,

I just looked for a wrench that looked as if it could be hammered on. I found one made out of heavy-duty metal with a broad end that could receive a blow. Sorting out the tools was, to me, just a process of observation and deduction.

At first the men took tools out of my hands and sent me on clean-up duties as they had Val. I would be told to clean up the hundreds of tools in the tool chest, just as she was. I would spend an entire day taking the tools out, wiping them down with a cleaner, lubricating them with grease, and putting them where they belonged. It was necessary work, and someone had to do it. But when I was finished with the cleaning, I insisted that the gang members clean up the tools before they replaced them. I refused to let them waste my time and insisted that "feminine" clean-up duties be rotated among other members.

I gave Valerie plenty of advice about how to stand up for herself. Once she was lead-off hand in a gang that was doing repairs on a platform I was responsible for. I saw her try to exert authority and her gang pusher stand up for her. A contract worker nicknamed Ivan refused to follow an order she had given.

She said, "Ivan, I'm the lead-off hand in this gang, and you'll do what I tell you to do."

Ivan said, "I'll throw you overboard before I'll follow your orders."

Dock, the gang pusher, came out of the barge cabin and collared Ivan. "You'll listen to her—and if you can't listen to her, because she's the only help I have right now—I'll take you to the boat and you can go home."

If Dock hadn't been there, Ivan might actually have thrown her overboard. Or she would have cried. Valerie's tears flowed more easily than mine. That lost her status among the men.

123

If she got emotionally distraught on a work location, they would let her take a boat back to the quarters to wash her face and compose herself. I, unlike Valerie, would never let them see me cry. To my mind, I was in a hostile environment with hard-hearted men on the lookout for signs of weakness, as they judged weaknesses. I never gave them the satisfaction of seeing my tears.

If a subordinate refused an order of mine, I let my boss handle it, if he was around, or I grabbed the worker by the scruff of the neck and took him to the barge cabin, where I told him to just sit and eat lunch or read magazines until the boss returned. I didn't get into power contests with the men who defied my authority. I let the command structure work for me.

Valerie was a woman who had never really had the opportunity to learn how to exert authority in a male-dominated setting. In a home where personal ties are the basis of relationship, tears, which are just one way of openly expressing emotions, may play a role in influencing people. She may not have learned other techniques for exerting influence. She had never had supervisory roles in any previous jobs. Shell had never trained her in supervisory skills. So Valerie not only had to face men who resented her presence in their men-only work force, she had to learn skills of command that I had learned in the Air Force. She was taking on a lot when she sought employment at East Bay. I did my best to warn her.

Because of her growing negativity about being on a work gang and the supervisors' perception of her as a safety hazard, the bosses began to move her into other less labor-intensive positions as they became available. One of the positions was as lease operator, the backbone of the oil operation. She was certainly capable of doing the work. However, she really didn't like the solitude and the responsibility of the job. One morning the person who had been training her for the past three weeks was called away on a different assignment, and she was told that she had to go out by herself to pull the charts, take readings, and do the paperwork on the platform that she had been training on. This task involved driving a boat to the location and reading some charts and meters. She refused. "What if something goes wrong? What if the platform blows up or something?"

"Well, you get on the radio and you call someone to help you," her supervisor said.

She still balked.

Her supervisor then offered to send another worker with her.

"Well, if you send him with me, then I'm in charge," she insisted.

This was certainly contradictory behavior. She refused the responsibility of the job but wanted to claim the authority of the supervisory position. So her boss just told her to go stay in the quarters until shift change and left the job undone for that day.

Unfortunately, in shifting her job assignment they moved her into positions that had usually been filled according to seniority or a gradual rise through the ranks. For example, the lease operator level usually followed Maintenance levels B and A. Rising through these levels often took years; my assignment to temporary lease operator came only after three years. This job-shifting was an unusual way to treat ineffective workers, who would either be let go or be assigned even less responsibile work, such as painting the docks or cleaning equipment. So Valerie was resented by some other longer-time workers.

The production foreman, John Town, claimed that by accomodating Valerie he was proving that he did not discriminate against women. I had different notions. I thought that preferential treatment was the most bigoted thing he could do. Instead, to learn the skills the job required, Valerie needed a different kind of training and support than the traditional new oil production employee, I thought. While most newly hired men were introduced to tools and mechanical procedures in high school, someone like Valerie would more likely have been required to take home economics. So more than on-the-job training and my coaching were needed. Also, workers like Valerie needed some training in social skills to help them assert their authority over males who respect power and defiance. Finally, the men themselves and their supervisors ought to have been trained in the problems associated with women in non-traditional work assignments and taught more constructive ways to integrate women into the blue-collar work force.

Ultimately, I believe, a woman who takes a non-traditional job must be willing to do the same tasks as any other new employee and must not demand that the rules change to accommodate her. If her upper body is too weak, she should work out with weights to improve it; I did this every other night after my shift. If she isn't strong enough to do a certain job, she should work smarter, finding tools and equipment to help her. Women who move into non-traditional, blue-collar jobs are taking on a tremendous physical and emotional challenge in the work itself—even more reason to protect them from harassment by co-workers.

The changes in job assignment didn't improve Valerie's situation. And the last job assignment change cost her my friendship and respect as well.

Valerie had been campaigning actively for an office job for at least a year when a new data processing job was created. She wanted this job, which would take her out of the oil fields and into the air-conditioned office at central facilities, where she would spend the day at a computer terminal putting in data.

Older men just five years from retirement, men who had been working as lease operators for years and whose bones and skin were worn out by the demands of sea and sand, also wanted that "soft" job to coast on. Seniority alone ought not to be the sole consideration in offering a worker a promotion, since not every oil production worker could be trained to do data processing on a computer. However, a very intelligent man with seventeen years with the company had also asked for the job and was well suited to it. But the supervisor, John Town, gave the data processing position to Valerie, a woman and a squeaky wheel. I thought it was unfair and, indeed, sexist to place a woman in a clerical job over the heads of suitable men.

Val and I fought angrily about it one night. I told her that in my opinion she ought to refuse the position. I thought it was bad for women to take advantages they hadn't earned. But she didn't care; she wanted to get off the work gang. For months later, I didn't speak to Valerie; what did we have in common, anyway? I felt ashamed to see a woman get coffee and dough-nuts and distribute newspapers to the men in her office.

Jenny's work history was similar to Valerie's. From the very first, Shell's decision to hire Jenny to work offshore had puzzled me. She seemed far too young and naive to handle a work

127

setting with 175 men and just two women. She was only nineteen, a product of a conservative Catholic upbringing in New Orleans, and had never been away from home before in her life. In fact, she was still a virgin. She was inexperienced in manual labor, too. Perhaps Jenny had been set up to fail at East Bay.

Even before Valerie began having trouble on the work gangs, Jenny was. From her first day at East Bay Jenny resisted doing the physically demanding, uncomfortable tasks assigned to work gang members. Within a few week-long hitches she was reassigned to the gas and oil sales station, where she would help load the oil barges that took the oil up the Mississippi to the refinery. The job entailed taking measurements and keeping records of the oil shipped from East Bay—very important work—but no work in the swamps or in open water. Unfortunately, the shift for gas and oil sales workers began at 4:00 A.M., and rising at 3:30 proved impossible for Jenny. She always overslept, even when co-workers arranged to tap on her window to make sure she was awake. According to her evaluations, when she did arrive she was not alert and efficient. Valerie and I spent hours coaxing and cajoling her to be more responsible. Neither of us wanted to see her fail because her failure would be a blow to the group of us.

But our help didn't work. Within two months Jenny was summoned to the operations foreman's office and given the warning: "Just because you are a woman doesn't mean we won't fire you. If your work doesn't improve, we will send you to the bank"—which was the phrase that meant "give you your final check." The bosses transferred her one final time and gave her three months to show progress.

Her job was clearly in jeopardy.

Jenny's final reassignment was to the warehouse, a climate-controlled environment where she placed orders for equipment most of the day. This is where she finally flourished. She got along with her co-worker, and her job performance quickly improved. However, in the insecure period just after she had been reassigned, Jenny was approached by "Dex" Pace, a Bottom Hole Pressure Analyst, who told her he could help her protect her job. Dex was the best friend of Roy Barker, Operation Foreman at East Bay. In effect, Jenny's job security came with a price tag: sleep with a friend of the boss and we'll take care of you.

Dex Pace was a married man twenty years older than Jenny. He had wide-set blue eyes, thinning brown hair, and a love of telling jokes. He was also rumored to be a heavy drinker. Jenny accepted the suggestion, and before long she and Dex were spending evenings out on fishing boats together. His visits to her room in our building eventually came to last all night. Once I walked into Jenny's room to talk with her and discovered them making love. In surprise, Dex rose up in bed and hit his back against a lamp attached to the wall above the bed, hurting himself deeply enough to leave a scar. Later, after Jenny had filed her grievance, I reminded Dex Pace that I knew about the scar and threatened to use it as evidence if he tried to deny his association with Jenny.

From the beginning of this affair I tried to talk Jenny out of it. I had always harkened to the good ole' Kentucky advice, "Don't get your honey and your money from the same pot." This folk wisdom had served me well for two years; while rumors flew that I was sleeping with one person or another, I could remain unperturbed, knowing that no one had ever seen me with anyone in that way. And these rumors were vicious, too. One day as I was walking through the foyer into the theatre for a safety meeting, I saw two three-foot-tall metal sculptures of a male and a female nude. One bore my name and the other had the name of the gang pusher I was working for at the time. Some welder had made them and placed them there to humiliate me. To the chagrin of the pranksters, I walked right by as if I hadn't even seen the disgusting things. But if I had been sleeping with my gang pusher, I might not have been able to retain my composure. When men tried to force themselves on me, as several did, I always told them I was a married women and wasn't interested.

Jenny wasn't married, though, and she lacked the experience to teach her what a bad idea it was to sleep with her co-workers. Both she and Val started affairs within the first week of work, and by their sixth hitch they'd found out that both men were married. In disappointment Valerie had wised up and stopped dating while offshore. Jenny, however, continued to have affairs.

Jenny was initially embarassed about the relationship with Dex, but she eventually fell in love with him. Although he was married, he fed her the lie that he would divorce his wife. After she began to press him to act on his promise, he changed his mind, though. In fact, when she found herself pregnant, he threatened to take the baby away from her and raise it himself. She miscarried in the second month. He also began beating her. When I discovered he had become violent, I stuck my neck out on her behalf.

One Monday noon hour I came across her in the bathroom. She was crying. When I asked her what was wrong, she told me the story of her date with Dex that weekend. She and Dex had been travelling with another Shell worker in a truck along a Louisiana interstate with Jenny at the wheel. She and Dex were arguing. He hit her and pressed her accelerator foot down with his foot until they had careened down the highway at almost 100 miles an hour. With her left foot on the brake, she was able to bring them to a stop. Then he beat her again and tried to throw her out of the truck. She was still very upset about the danger and abuse she'd faced that weekend. I was upset myself, and as soon as I heard her out, I told her, "I'll go have a talk with him."

I strode right over to his office and charged inside.

"You should leave Jenny alone. She's much too young for you, and besides, you've been feeding her a bunch of lies."

"You don't know what you're talking about," he hissed. "And besides, it's none of your business. Close the door behind you."

I threw him a warning as I left: "Some day you'll be sorry for this."

Jenny was heartbroken over Dex's refusal to divorce his wife and marry her. Her job performance at the warehouse, which had been good for two years, deteriorated because of the emotional pressure she was under, and complaints were filed. As I saw it, Jenny was a very inexperienced young woman in waters way over her head.

Gradually, Jenny began pulling away from Dex Pace and dating another man at East Bay. This brought the wrath of Dex and his friends down on her. They began to circle her like a pack of wolves creeping around a downed deer. Dex became even more violent toward her. At the same time, Dex's friend, Roy Barker, began to threaten to fire her. He'd been her immediate supervisor when she and Dex got together, and he still had indirect authority over her. Several times I saw him shake his finger at her and say, "You had better get your fuckin' mind on your job." Roy was keeping a file on her work performance and had been influencing her job evaluations all along.

In one move against Jenny, Roy Barker rounded up five of the six operations foremen and took them the sixteen miles up river to the boat terminal, where they all met with the head of the Purchasing Department to complain about mistakes in Jenny's orders for tools, parts, and equipment. Only one of the operations foremen refused to go along with the witch hunt Roy Barker organized. This operations foreman said that he had no complaints against Jenny, and the others were just harassing her. I think he was the only honest man among them.

Jenny's warehouse job included ordering new equipment, parts, and tools needed by the operations foremen. She was supposed to be able to compare the foreman's requisition form with items in equipment catalogs. If a foreman's order was so vague she had trouble finding the item in the catalog, she was supposed to call him up on the phone and confirm his order before sending money to vendors and having the materials brought. If she failed to double-check with the foreman, she might end up ordering the wrong tool or flange. That's what Roy Barker kept accusing her of. Actually, during this period she might not have been making those phone calls. Who would want to call men who were trying to intimidate her? She avoided contact with many superiors if she could, even having her helper carry paperwork to the main office instead of going up there herself. But who could blame her when she was so obviously being persecuted?

Roy Barker's malice included announcements at his morning meetings with his gang pushers about how he planned to get Jenny that day. For instance, one morning he assigned someone the duty of watching the dock where Jenny and her assistant William were supposed to leave the oxygen and acetylene tanks used for welding to be picked up and refilled. Since Roy hadn't seen them on the dock as he arrived for the meeting, he was sure Jenny was going to make another mistake, and he wanted someone to be there to pounce on her if she did. Some of the gang pushers began to stop by the warehouse to warn Jenny of what Roy planned for her that day. Her helper, William, was also an ally. Since he worked side-by-side with her, he witnessed the vendetta sparked by her rejection of Dex Pace, and his sense of justice was outraged. When Jenny filed a lawsuit, William quit his job so that he could testify on her behalf.

Not every woman's career at East Bay suffered from combining work with pleasure as Jenny's had. Nancy, the production clerk at East Bay, was the best example of that. However, because Nancy's situation differed in several important respects from Jenny's, Nancy was never as vulnerable as Jenny or the rest of us. Most important, Nancy was protected by the nature of her work location. The office on the island was a relatively civilized space where she came into contact only with a limited set of people. We women on work gangs, on the other hand, encountered boat drivers, Coast Guard, other work gangs—a wide array of oil production employees and workers in related industries. In Nancy's office, people were usually around who would witness any sexual harassment, whereas Jenny, Valerie, and I were sometimes alone or with just one male co-worker when he mooned, flashed, or touched us. Also, Nancy was doing clerical work, a traditionally female occupation since the turn of the century. As a result, she did not earn the animosity from territorial, traditionalist males that we non-traditional female hard-hats did. Nancy, of course, was the victim of the same cruel humor that the rest of us were. Polish sausages with notes saying "Suck this!" or some other obscenity were left on her desk. Still, her job did have some advantages that Jenny's job did not have.

While Jenny from the outset had not tackled the work with a will, Nancy's job performance was above reproach. She was one of those strong-willed, competent organizers who are often said to be running the whole shebang. People used to say that the production foremen at East Bay were afraid of her.

Nancy had been working at East Bay for about six months by the time I was hired as a blue-collar worker. Since she and I were on opposite crews, we got to know one another only through brief conversations on Thursdays, when she was taking the boat back to land and I had just arrived, or vice versa. We arranged matching bedspreads for our two bunks and shared the cost of a small TV set for the room. A solid-built woman of about thirty-eight with a pretty face and hairdo, she had been a production clerk on the Alaska pipeline before coming to the damp delta country.

In both her past and present positions Nancy claimed the right to fraternize as she chose. And she did. In fact, Nancy seemed to see men as a job benefit, along with health coverage and vacation. But Nancy was discreet and kept her personal life from blending with her professional life more successfully than Jenny had. I couldn't fault her. Her affairs brought her deep personal sorrow, though.

Nancy fell for a man who was married. Their relationship was none of my business—I never asked her about it, and she never told me—but I knew it must be torrid, because I had evidence. I discovered at the beginning of my shift one week that my bed had been "pipe locked." Pipe lock is a kind of metallic-based glue for metal joints. According to the gossip, my bed had collapsed while Nancy and her lover had been having sex on it.

Nancy believed that this man was going to marry her. His marriage was in trouble, probably because of his philandering, and his wife was enraged. On her weeks off Nancy sometimes rented a motel room in her lover's town so that he and she could spend nights together. One evening his wife came to the motel and blew down the door with a shotgun. Nancy was able to escape that night, and her lover separated from his wife and got an apartment in the same town.

On the day Nancy and her lover had set for their marriage ceremony, he disappeared, and the disappointment shattered her. She had a nervous breakdown and spent six weeks in the psychiatric unit of a hospital. His desertion hit her entirely by surprise. For two months Nancy had been carrying home her house plants, her extra bath towels, and other decorative do-dads week by week, expecting that after the ceremony she would not be returning to work. I even bought out her half of our jointly-owned TV set. When Nancy didn't return for her next shift, I thought everything had gone according to her plan. However, her psychiatrist, who called to make sure that no one from Shell tried to get in touch with Nancy, told us her unhappy story.

Almost two months later Nancy still hadn't heard from her lover. She returned to work and began to piece together evidence of an affair that he had been carrying on simultaneously with theirs. From the long-distance phone records out of East Bay, she deduced that when he left her bed at 4:00 A.M. he'd been calling a woman other than his wife who also lived in his home town. She'd assumed that he'd been getting ready for early morning meetings.

When Nancy returned to work, recovered but still on anti-depressants, Shell Oil reassigned her to the night shift, a reassignment she did not like. The night assignment included periodic inspections of the property and marina with only a flashlight and responding to dangerous changes in weather. As a production clerk, Nancy had never done that kind of outdoor work, and she didn't want to do it. However, the man she had trained to fill in for her wanted to keep her position. The supervisors let him stay and reassigned Nancy, telling her that the reassignment was "in the company's best interest." As a salaried employee without a union, she had no alternative but to go along with it. All of her competence as production clerk had not earned her the support and loyalty of her supervisors.

So Nancy, still unmarried, worked for two more years and began another affair with another Shell employee, a divorced man, who eventually married her. When she finally left she filed a grievance with the Equal Employment Opportunity Commission and won the right to sue, but she backed down for lack of funds and fear for her husband's position with Shell.

April was hired onto Nancy's crew in 1983, offering Nancy the same opportunity for a female friend after hours that I had enjoyed when Valerie and Jenny were hired. Unfortunately,

Nancy didn't like April and spread the word that April was just plain dumb. April was hired as a laborer on a work gang in spite of the fact that she was very thin—five feet eight inches tall and 115 pounds—and inexperienced. A woman in her late twenties, April had spent all her years caring for her mother and her numerous pets in a very small town on the Mississippi Gulf coast. From the outset, the work required more strength than she had, so, although her weekly evaluations always approved her for trying hard, they were usually negative. In the first three weeks of work April suffered an elbow injury that put her on sick leave for six weeks and then on light office duty for months later. During this time when April was working in the office under Nancy's supervision, Nancy became very critical of April.

The office work led to a transfer that worked out well for April, though. While helping out there she came into contact with Lamar, the head of the surveying department. This amiable Cajun knew his job as well as anyone at East Bay and had run the department very successfully for years. However, many of us who had seen him work suspected he didn't know how to read. Lamar was very eager to recruit someone who could learn surveying techniques and equipment and, secretly, cover for his illiteracy. April was interested, and the gang pushers, who had been disgruntled by her injury and her lack of strength, supported the transfer. As an added benefit, April would no longer work during the same weeks as Nancy but would be part of the "B" crew with Jenny, Valerie, and me.

April's performance in the surveying department was exceptional. She picked up the technical skills quickly and was especially good at the drafting. Lamar, her supervisor, appreciated her talents and worked well with her. Moving and setting

137

up surveying instruments didn't require the brute strength and endurance of oil jacket and pipeline repairs, so it was was more suited to her frail frame. Still, April's lack of physical hardiness eventually caught up with her: after three years of success as a land survey crew member, April died of pneumonia during one of her weeks off from work. Her mother found her dead in her bed.

All the women at East Bay endured the same kind of sexual harassment and job discrimination that I did. We shared stories of our experiences daily and were even able to notice subtle differences in the way our co-workers harassed us. For example, Jenny was mooned more frequently than I was. One boat captain regularly pulled down his pants and exposed his hind-quarters to her whenever he rode by the shipping dock where she worked. Once the foreman caught him exposing himself and rebuked him soundly for it. He asked Jenny if she wanted to put the man on report, but she shrugged the suggestion off. This man's rear end had become such a familiar sight to Jenny that she had become utterly indifferent to it. We'd all learned to pick and choose our battles; she would save her reports for the big stuff.

I myself witnessed one man try to humiliate her by flashing her. After returning by boat from a work location, she and I had docked at the living quarters. I stayed behind to tie up the boat while she began walking along the catwalk to the build-ings. I looked up when I heard a male voice yell "Hey, Jenny," and saw a nude man step out of a doorway not more than fifteen feet from her. He didn't notice that I was there, and he must have thought he could get away with the attempt at humiliation without witnesses.

By witnessing one another's experiences, we women were

able to support and sustain one another as we challenged the status quo. We all felt we had a right to the same work opportunities as men and were willing to do the job to our best ability. Some of us got more confused, more hurt, than others. Each one of us responded in our own way to the sexism we were facing. However, our combined experience showed us that certain general problems prevailed.

First, Shell repeatedly hired women as laborers who lacked the physical strength to do the work. Only those women strong enough for vigorous manual labor should be given the opportunity to work in offshore oil production. At the same time, women who take these jobs should have the fortitude to face the rigors of the work and the uncomfortable working conditions. Strength tests for all applicants, male or female, should be a part of the screening process.

Second, Shell hired people who lacked experience in manual labor and then failed to provide adequate training for them. On-the-job training by co-workers was an important component of training, but the male co-workers of the new female employees were more critical of the women's inexperience and offered them less information and patience than they would have offered a new, inexperienced male co-worker. The supervisors at East Bay ought to have persuaded the male employees to adopt a more helpful attitude. At the same time, the new women employees needed to be prepared to pick up what they could at every opportunity and be willing to ask questions, even at the risk of seeming stupid.

Another aspect of neglected training was in supervisory skills. Shell expected the women who were hired as Shell employees to supervise contract workers on work gangs without recognizing how the men's sexism would complicate the women's difficulty in assuming authority. At the same time the women lead-off hands needed to become more flexible, to employ machismo more, in order to establish their authority with their co-workers.

Ultimately, we women workers were thrust into a work environment that was unprepared to accept us. We were dropped into a pack of dogs, a society that was hostile, even life-threatening. And this hostility could easily have been predicted and compensated for.

For B.J., the experience of gender terrorism forced her to consider the ways she was both like and different from the stereotypes of women. She had always assumed that she had very little in common with other women and so never placed much credit in other women's testimony that they had been discriminated against. Because she had never personally experienced gender terrorism, B.J. did not believe that gender terrorism happens in the workplace. Her experience at East Bay taught her to understand that each woman, unique as she is, shares with every other woman the potential to be sexually harassed and discriminated against in the workplace.

When other women joined B.J. at East Bay, she was able to gain the support of confidantes and witnesses. By witnessing and validating one another's experiences, she and the other women at East Bay were able to support and sustain one another as they challenged the status quo. Just as B.J. had for two years, the other women at East Bay felt that they had a right to the same work opportunities as men. They were willing to do the job to their best ability. Admittedly, some of them got more confused and more entangled in the manipulations of gender terrorists than others, and each one of them would admit having made some mistakes. As was perfectly normal, each one of them responded in her own way to the gender terrorism she was facing.

In justice, however, a company ought to be accountable to its women employees for the hostile or dangerous working climate generated by its policies and practices.

To B.J.'s mind, Shell Oil seemed to be setting up the women they hired to fail. Besides refusing to recognize or respond to B.J.'s complaints of harassment and discrimination, they hired women far less physically hardy than B.J.; then they offered them insufficient training.

In justice, the company could have recognized how the men's sexism would complicate the women's difficulty in assuming authority. Instead of throwing the women into the alligator pit, the company could have offered them training in supervising resistant, hostile subordinates. The new female employees could have been taught ways to adopt a more authoritative style of supervision. The company seemed unwilling to face the reality of B.J.'s experience, leaving B.J. and each other woman to cope with gender terrorism as best she could.

IV
SUCCESS

❧

The drive to fulfill one's potential is one of the strongest forces in the human spirit. Any frustration of that drive takes its toll on the individual herself and on society in general. When a social pattern such as discrimination against women in the workplace blocks the energies of a whole group of people, the spirit of a whole society can slowly die. On the other hand, when individuals are offered just and equitable treatment, their drive to realize their potential can liberate a society's vitality.

8

TAKING CARE OF
MY PATIENTS: TRAINING
AS A LEASE OPERATOR

༄

Sexual harassment and discrimination suppress the joy of personal achievement and so are a blight on the life of an organization and even on a family and community. This was clearly true when the prejudiced attitudes of men at high levels blocked B.J.'s opportunities for advancement and development in the oil production industry. For longer than any of her co-workers, she was kept at the same low level of pay and responsibility while men she trained were promoted above her, even though her work evaluations were always excellent. An attitude of discrimination pervaded and soured the workplace.

When, through her persistence, B.J. was finally able to move into a job category that would offer new challenges and responsibilites and real independence, she was able to join a more technically-minded group of workers who felt less defensive of their manhood and more receptive to her as a coworker.

Nothing gives me such delight as to realize new potentials within myself. I have a strong need to be always striving, growing, and accomplishing more. The hard manual labor to build new structures or repair existing ones suited my spirit gloriously. I wanted more. I wanted to be the first woman lease operator in the Gulf of Mexico.

A lease operator is a person responsible for the production of oil and gas from a specified platform or group of platforms. A "lease" refers to a section of the waters for which the company has mineral rights. So the lease operator oversees the wells and platforms in a section and is thus the kingpin of the oil production industry. No woman had ever been entrusted with that responsibility by any oil company operating on the Gulf of Mexico.

My goal of being the first woman lease operator was as far away as it had been when I had formed it in 1980. At hiring, I was classified, like any other new worker, as Maintenanceman C, but the tag "New" was added to my classification just for me. After six months, the "New" was dropped, and a year later "C" was changed to "B." The track I wanted to follow was: Maintenanceman A, Lease Operator B, and then Senior Productions Operator. At that point a person might become an Operations Foreman, to be trained for a year by engineers onshore and then come back to East Bay to run a whole block

of leases. Each one of these levels would bring new responsibilities, challenges, knowledge, and, of course, pay.

When I was assigned to NAVAIDS, however, my classification was shifted to "Temporary Mechanic B." I didn't want
that job. "Mechanics" was a speciality that was a deadend.
But the work gang is a pool of temporary, fill-in laborers for
any of the specialities. Getting moved out of a work gang to
be trained in a speciality is definitely a promotion, and if work
gang members are asked to move into a specialty, they had
better accept if they ever want to move up at all. The word
"temporary" designates a trainee or someone transferred to a
certain kind of work for a brief period of time; "temporary"
people are ineligible for promotion.

Because I was designated "temporary," I figured that I was
not going to be in the NAVAIDS position for long. But I was
wrong. During the nine months I was stuck there, I trained
three people with less seniority and watched two of them get
transferred to better-paying jobs over my head. I felt that I had
been pushed into a job with enormous responsibility and not
even a permanent classification. The unfairness of it afflicted
me, and I felt trapped by it. I couldn't actively seek a reassignment because that meant making waves, and I didn't feel
secure enough in my job to do that. Also, getting passed over
for promotion was intimidating in itself. Still, when a third
trainee was assigned me, I told him, "Look, if someone moves
out of this position, it's going to be me, not you, Okay?"

I'd paid my dues and accomplished remarkable things. I'd
almost singlehandedly repaired the deteriorated NAVAIDS system, which was vital to the safety of the waterways. I'd thrown
myself into my work with a will, taking on physically difficult

tasks alongside my male co-workers and receiving weekly evaluations that often said, "B.J. gives 150 percent." I'd read all the manuals in the island's library, attended every Saturday-night training class held at the quarters, and badgered the instructor, Tom Bouvier, like a two-year old. He used to tell me in friendly exasperation, "You don't need to know everything about these wells to run the platform, B.J."

It was Tom Bouvier who helped me make my move, and it happened almost by accident. He was the instructor of the Saturday night classes because he was the Operations Foreman of Block 27, an area of leases in the deep waters almost sixteen miles off the barrier island where the living quarters were. Most of my NAVAIDS work was in this block, so he came to know me and to respect my eagerness to know more.

One class period he was discussing the NAVAIDS facilities and asked me what I thought about the position. I said, "Well, it's a good job, and it's a good-paying job for somebody, but I'm still a temporary mechanic, and I don't want to stay there. I don't even want to be a mechanic. I want to be a lease operator." The twenty people sitting in the classroom with us saw his surprise and heard him promise, "Okay, we'll see what we can do about it." I now realize that I was subconsciously readying myself for the opportunity Tom Bouvier provided. My goal was always in the back of my mind, so I was ready to jump when the first opportunity to ask for it occurred.

Tom Bouvier helped me by asking John Town, the Production Foreman, to transfer me to his Block 27. Within two weeks I turned over the NAVAIDS system to my well-pleased trainee, who was immediately promoted to a permanent mechanic position that earned higher pay than I had ever gotten. I took a two-dollar-an-hour pay cut back to Maintenanceman

B—they never did make me Maintenanceman A—and began to "trail" a senior lease operator by the name of Beaudioux.

Beaudioux had been a lease operator for twenty years. A Cajun with more culinary flair than Paul Prudhomme, he could also run an oil platform as well as anyone in the business, and, more important for me, he knew how to teach as well. He was patient, explaining each complicated gauge, manifold, or panel clearly. He knew that my "book learning" in Shell's training programs would take me only so far on an oil platform, so he offered me lots of experience—the best teacher. He would point me toward a task, explain it, then send me to execute it. "But if you're not sure of what you are doing," he would warn, "don't do it. Come ask." He lent me notebooks to study after hours and, when I was having trouble picking up on the complicated paperwork, he went over it carefully with me and answered all my questions. Thriving under his pleasant mentorship, I learned enough about the platform to handle it by myself on the third week.

I was being trained on a platform known as "J." (Letters of the alphabet were used to designate oil platforms; since the number of platforms far exceeded the number of letters available, some platforms had double or even triple letter designations, as "J" was connected by catwalk to platform "JJ." "JJJ," nearby, was reached by boat.) Platforms are really like the knots in a network of lace. Pipes from wells in an area all come in to a platform (or constellation of platforms like "J," "JJ," and "JJJ"), bringing together the oil and gas that have been brought to the surface at the wells. The platforms harbor a system of high-, intermediate- and low-pressure systems, testing vessels, and calibration equipment. Ordinarily, an automatic system controls the flow through the platform, but a lease operator needs to know how to control the flow manually by being able to read flow and pressure gauges and adjust the appropriate valves. Platform "J" was half the size of a football field, four stories (or about eighty feet) high, and it collected oil and gas from forty-five wells.

Platform "J" also pumped water into injector wells throughout Block 27 by means of its "waterflood system," which was on the top level. The waterflood system extracts salt water from an underground reservoir of salt water and removes sand and dissolved gas. Three pumps run by jet turbine engines build up the pressure in stages to 1,400 pounds per square inch, and then they inject the water down into the oil reservoir 5,000 to 17,000 feet below to replace the oil and gas that have been drawn out. The waterflood system thus maintains the pressure in the vast underground chambers.

My nurse's training helped me find a way to understand the waterflood system; it was like the circulatory system in the human body. The valves of the wells kept the fluid flowing in just one direction, just as the valves in human veins and arteries do. The jet engines and pumps were the heart of the waterflood system. They were formidable pieces of equipment, powerful enough to lift an airplane full of passengers to 35,000 feet, or, in this case, to drive water about 17,000 feet below. As in the human body, a certain pressure in the system—not too much and not too little—meant optimal performance.

I would have to understand the equipment and the principles behind their operation. Once fully trained as a lease operator, I would work mostly alone on an assigned platform. Although a mechanic would ordinarily be available to help, I would need to be able to respond to emergencies, so I had to learn how to start the engines and pumps and to shut down the waterflood system. This last was no small task. As anyone who has siphoned a gas tank or waterbed knows, once a self-contained system of liquids begins to flow it doesn't want to stop.

I knew when I had asked for the job that many people had failed lease operator training. Throughout this training period I was anxious that I, too, might fail. At East Bay, those who failed as lease operators were called "dumb." The word stirred up painful echoes of my parents calling me me dumb because I studied all the time. I feared hearing the word applied to me if I failed as a lease operator.

Fortunately, my apprehensions were soon eased. In my third week on Platform "J" I was able to prove to myself and to others how my innate talent for this kind of work combined with reasoning skills and experience to help me solve a problem on my own. Beaudioux was taking a week of vacation, and I was responsible for "J" all by myself. Repairs to the waterflood system had been ordered, and the day for the maintenance gang's work had arrived. As operator of the platform I was supposed to shut down the waterflood system. I had to close off the water coming from the source wells, then let the pressure drop until I could shut down the engines.

I executed the procedure methodically, following the step-by-step notes I'd taken while Beaudioux had trained me. Something was wrong. Gauges indicated that the pressure hadn't dropped in the low-pressure separator. I pored over my notes, tracing my steps again and again. Puzzled and frustrated, I was finally forced to admit that I was doing everything according to instructions. Then I began to think through the instructions themselves. Was everything in my notes logical? Had some step been left out that logically needed to be completed? I walked myself through the lines and valves again, muttering to myself an explanation of the way each valve or fitting worked to achieve the ultimate result. I was able to eliminate certain possibilities and finally focused in on one valve as the probable source of the problem. I investigated. Eureka! I discovered that a valve had been put in backwards, thus preventing that area of the system from going to normal pressure. That valve had been replaced the week before, while I was off.

So I'd found the problem; now I had to find a solution. With pressure still in the system, work could not proceed safely. The maintenance gang had already arrived and was goofing off in the dog shack. Would I be able to prove myself? Pressure! I very much wanted to earn a good reputation as a lease operator trainee.

I found a release valve and connected it by a high-pressure hose to a low-pressure vessel. From there I could route the gas and water far away from the platform. In that way I was able to bleed the system down to atmospheric pressure through another self-contained vessel.

Exhilaration and pride surged through me at the completion of this job. I had understood the basics of a very complicated platform and felt confident that I would easily meet the future challenges of lease operation.

Working with the equipment was thrilling to me. As I stood before the vast array of gauges on Platform "J" I recalled my first exposure to a waterflood system in my first week of work years before. For some reason, I'd been awakened in the middle of the night to go out to Waterflood #5 to help with a repair. I still have no idea why I was selected to go; I had no experience with the work. When we got there, the mechanic, an old and very small man, was already hard at work. He was very slow, methodical, and thorough in his explanations.

I was in a daze, though, and not really getting it. I'd been asleep, it was dark, and I didn't know anything about the waterflood system. When he completed the repairs, though, he let me push the "On" switch. I was like a four-year-old child, utterly hooked from that moment on. If you do the repairs right, these huge jet airplane engines will jump into motion. Now as a lease operator trainee years later, I was also understanding why those engines worked. This sensation of elation in my own powers sustained me through every difficulty.

During this training period I was also adopted into the circle of lease operators, a friendly family who accepted me as an equal. In the late afternoon the lease operators would meet at one of the platforms for an informal gathering before returning at shift's end to the living quarters on the island. Our discussions would range widely from work projects to attitudes about supervisors to personal problems. Although the gossip network at East Bay buzzed with secrets, I never heard anything that had been revealed during these afternoons repeated outside our circle. We offered one another that confidentiality.

With Beaudioux as a companionable teacher and this new circle of co-workers, I felt more comfortable at East Bay. Often enough, however, I was confronted by men who questioned my judgement or who were angry about my authority to order repairs from work gangs and other maintenance workers. One was Raymond, a paraffin cutter. Much as cholesterol builds up inside veins and arteries of the human body, paraffin builds up in the pipes that extend deep through water and earth into the reservoirs below. Paraffin cutters ream out the paraffin with snake-like rotating knives. If the flow from a well has dropped gradually, it's time for a paraffin cutter to clear out the pipe.

Although still a temporary lease operator I was assigned to cover "J" and "S" platforms for someone on vacation. One day I called for a boat to take me from "J" to "S." When the boat arrived, I was glad to see Raymond aboard because a nearby well needed "cutting." As I was talking to the boat captain about what I needed in the "S" platform area, Raymond was sitting there but not facing me. To get his attention and get him engaged in the discussion, I tapped lightly on his hard hat with my clipboard. After all, since he was assigned to work on "J" and "S," he was supposed to give me whatever help I asked for. When I tapped his hat, however, he erupted. He jumped up from his perch and slapped me hard across the face. My lip split open painfully, and blood flowed freely. "No woman ever does that to me, and don't you forget it," he roared like a crazy man. The captain quickly picked up a big wrench and thrust it toward me for protection, but I waved it away. Shell's policy was to fire both parties in a fight, regardless of who started it, so I was sure to lose my job if I took him on. And I'd already been told about Raymond, his hair-trigger temper, his excitability, and his wife-abusing. He was clearly deranged, as I saw it. Why fight with a madman? I wiped the blood from my mouth and dropped my plans for cutting the well. I would never call on him for assistance again.

My training took me to several other platforms to "trail" several other lease operators. From Ronald on Platform "K" I learned how to keep valves and other moving parts made of metal in top condition in spite of the corroding salt water. Whenever we took the boat from well to well, we also carried an oil can and grease gun. While we were there, we lubricated everything. Almost all other operators believed that good maintenance like this was futile, but Ronald made it happen. And his preventive medicine minimized shut-downs, which cost dollars in time, materials, and lost production. Ronald was considered by everyone to be an outstanding lease operator.

After training at a series of platforms in Block 27, Tom Bouvier's block, I eventually ran several of them myself while their regular operators were on vacation. But soon I was reassigned from Block 27, regarded by most operators as the best block, to Block 24, the area just three miles from the barrier island. This was the least desirable of the lease operation assignments, but the supervisors told me that this block would offer the next lease operator's position.

Block 24 was in state-controlled waters rather than federal waters, so I had to learn new procedures to comply with state laws. Since the waters of this marshland were shallower than the open water I'd been working in before, the equipment and platforms were on a smaller scale. No longer did I have to call up a larger boat, called a lugger, when I wanted to be taken from platform to platform. I got a jo-boat of my own instead. Of course, I was responsible for maintaining it—something I'd learned while on work gangs.

What I hadn't learned about, though, was navigation. In this desolate, tranquil marsh at the edge of sea and land, fog could materialize as suddenly as a ghost. It would billow off the water and embrace me until I felt myself to be floating in an unearthly dimension. I felt bereft of north, south, east, and west, bereft of the margins beyond the gunwales of the boat, bereft of time itself. The fog might roll in at six in the evening, cling to the area all night, and then let go its hold in the morning's sun. Or it might be stubborn. Once a layer of fog blanketed the area for two weeks. If the fog blanket were thin, the light from the sun would bounce around inside the cloud, blinding me with its intense whiteness. Once the layer was so thin that I was above it at the top of a forty-foot platform. From my perch I surveyed a vast field of billows, as if I were suddenly in the midst of a field of freshly fallen snow.

The fogs of the Mississippi delta were awesome—and fear is one ingredient in awe's recipe. Navigating my jo-boat in the fog, especially at night, terrified me. Each boat was equipped with radar so that we could navigate even when the fog surrounded us, but I was offered no training with the equipment. To use the radar, I had to lean my face forward into a rubber boot that would reduce glare on the round readout screen. The intersection of the crosshairs would mark my position, and white blips on the screen would indicate obstacles, banks, and structures. It was crazy. I much preferred to follow the haunting sound of a foghorn to my destination. If I was on my way to a manned platform, I radioed ahead and asked those on the platform to turn on their foghorn, and I would follow its call.

Training on the marshy state land took me into another interesting realm—the past. I was introduced to the antique oil wells that had been in operation ever since the region was opened up to oil production. Some of these wells were thirty years old, and the equipment had been obsolete for two decades.

This new location challenged me far more than the platforms in more open water had. First of all, these wells and platforms were accessible only by a maze of canals that had been dredged in the marshes. I was expected to learn how to find each one of the hundred oil-, gas-, and water-injector wells associated with Platforms "B," "BB," "D," and "H," and Waterflood #5. And second, each well was different—some new, some old, some producing at predictable rates, some inconstant and unpredictable. I was overwhelmed with more information than I could take in at one time, and I had to find a way to organize it. So I began to associate this lease with a hospital and to think of each well as a patient.

Patients and wells are all individuals with locations, complaints, and needs specific to them. Just as a patient is in a particular room in a hospital, a well lies along a certain canal. Just as a patient has a certain medical condition, a well has a specific engineering problem. Just as a patient needs certain medication, a well needs certain maintenance. In the hospital I'd learned to associate names with faces and conditions, and in the marsh I learned to make similar associations.

"B," "BB," and their associated platforms were operated by two full-time operators working together on day shifts and a single person on nights. Two were older men a couple of years from retirement. The third was the notorious Nick Claire, the first man to harass me at East Bay.

On my first afternoon of work at East Bay in January of 1980, I'd been sent down into a deep, water-filled hole to help repair a broken water line. Nick had been working right beside me. After we completed the job and were waiting out a brief rainstorm, he told me that I must be a whore or a husband-hunter to want to work at East Bay. After that I worked in a gang with him for several months. Although he had only six months more seniority, he'd been promoted far more rapidly than I and at this time was two grade levels above me. He'd already been a Lease Operator B for six months.

In my opinion, Nick was a petty, mean-spirited man. Nothing proved this to me more clearly than an incident that took place a year and a half earlier on the EB2, a "lay-barge" (one

157

designed to lay pipelines), when he pushed me aside in order to take credit for work I did.

On that occasion Shell Oil workers on the EB2 were competing with contract workers on the "Torch 2" to lay four-inch pipe—miles and miles of it. We were starting out from different locations and were to connect our ends at Platform E. We two lay-barges had worked up a rivalry: just like those railroad workers who laid the transcontinental rail lines in the nineteenth century, we were going to see which group could work the hardest and fastest.

When pipe is laid, sections have to be fitted and welded together. This work is done on the barge. As the pipe sections are joined, a boat on the front end of the barge pulls the new length off into the water. This kind of work is probably some of the most physically demanding work in the oil field. It also requires the best teamwork, expecially between the workers who are joining the pipe sections.

Joining pipe requires a team of three: the welder, the pipe fitter, and the welder helper. As a new joint between pipe sections is begun, the welder helper moves a thirty-foot pipe section into place with a crane. The pipe fitter who is standing there gets the ends butted together. A bevel on the pipe is cut to fit one end to the other. Then the welder begins to move around the circumference of the pipe, melting the rod of welding metal with an electric current to seal the joint. The rough surfaces of slag have to be ground off with a disc grinder, leaving a clean seal. That is the welder helper's job, too. The work requires lots of lifting, careful adjustments of position, and attention to what the other two workers are doing. When a team works. together smoothly, that means something, and my team was doing it.

The EB2 carried another welding team so that joints at both ends of a pipe section could be sealed at the same time. We were doing lots of pipe every day, all day long. We got breaks only when the boss on the boat decided to stop pulling line off the barge. It was hard, hot, heavy labor. But our drive to beat the "Torch 2" and be the best kept us moving through our fatigue.

When we got hooked up with the "Torch 2" after three days of this back-straining work, one weld was left to be made, and it was being done by the welder I was working with. I was ready with the grinder to finish off the slag that would mark the end of the job. Getting to bring our team to victory was a real charge for me. I was standing there with a big grin on my face waiting to move in when the welder helper from the other welding team, which had already finished and was standing watching us finish the job, came over and grabbed the grinder out of my hand. "Here," he said, "I'll finish it. You go put the tools away."

That was Nick Claire.

"No!" I insisted, grabbing at my grinder. "This is my welder, and I'll do it."

As we were squabbling over the handtool like two brats in a sandbox, Slade Mead, my boss, intervened. "Give him the grinder, B.J."

He drew me away from Nick, took me by the shoulder and said, "I know this is wrong, but he's a man, and he wants to show off in front of those guys on 'Torch 2.' Let him do it."

That was hard to take. I had spent the last three days working as hard as I ever had in my life, only to have my boss step in and let that little worm Nick take my tool out of my hand and the credit away from me. Just because he was a man and I

159

was a woman, I was expected to step aside. I had as much pride in my work as any man, as large an ego, and as much a right to glory as he did. Yet I was expected to be a bigger person than Nick was. And I guess I was, because I said to Slade Mead—with a lot of resentment in my voice, I'll admit—"Okay, what the hell do you want me to do next?"

Nick's pettiness was evident when I trailed him during those shifts on Platform "B" as well. Usually, when two people worked as a team, they would trade off the more physically-taxing jobs: "I'll jump out of the rocking boat onto the well jackets one day, and you do it the next." Not with Nick. He assigned me all the dirty work and, since he was in charge, what he said went. He even had me working his night shifts all by myself, even though I was supposedly not completely trained. To his mind I was taking a job away from a man, so his dislike was unrelenting. To my mind, Nick Claire was the cruel stepmother, and I was Cinderella.

Fortunately, even Cinderella got to go to the ball. I did, too.

Shell Oil Company threw banquets for employees and their spouses about twice a year. The banquets took place at elegant hotels in New Orleans, Biloxi, or Baton Rouge. One was upcoming, and Jerry and Tom, the two older men who operated Platform "B" along with Nick Claire, were urging me to attend. They were far kinder to me than Nick was. Jim and I used to sing songs at the top of our voices as we were boating from one location to another. I started to think that it might be fun to go to a party along with them. I explained my reluctance to them.

The first party I attended had been a very bad experience for me and for Joe, who'd accompanied me. For one thing,

I'd been told by my boss that if I attended, I couldn't drink. Now an open bar, along with free lodging and tickets to special events, was one of the chief attractions of these parties. Everyone who attended took liberal advantage of the open bar. I objected vigorously to the double standard.

"Don't invite me to a party where you can drink but I can't."

"Well, you can't curse."

"But you curse."

"Yeah, but we're going to be at a hotel."

"What do you think I am, some nitwit who doesn't know how to handle herself? I can drink, I can cuss, and I bet your wife does."

"Well, you're right about that."

"Don't expect me not to drink. In fact, I want to get falling down drunk, because that will make it easier to be around all of you."

I and Joe had gone to that party in spite of my boss. We went top-drawer, too. I wanted to look sexy, proud of my man and proud of myself. I had bought a three-hundred-dollar dress, had my hair done, and looked pretty good. But I was sorry that I'd exposed Joe to the humiliation I was suffering. When we each opened up our gifts from the company, we found that I'd been given a belt buckle and he'd been given a make-up mirror. I'd refused for six years to go back to another one.

Jerry and Tom were persistent, though. "We know you better now. Lots of people like you."

Joe and I went and were glad we did. We enjoyed the plush surroundings and the elegant meals provided by the company. I was invited to dance by Jerry and Tom and even some of the gang pushers I had worked for in the past, and Joe danced with some of their wives. This time, Joe's gift was two nice pieces of luggage. On our way back to Pensacola we took a walk along the beach and felt a pleasant glow. How different our experience was this time! Perhaps I was going to be able to feel at home at East Bay after all.

When Joe accompanied me to that second party, it was just one event in a gradual reconciliation that proceeded by fits and starts. Even after the divorce and the continuing manipulation of one another's feelings, we still felt that we were committed to one another.

Joe had been spending more of his time in his solitary cabin in the state forest. In fact, I'd picked him up there to take him to the Shell party. But his obsession with the end of the world had begun to worry me. Although it took a full month to get the telephone company to run a line out to that isolated location, I had a telephone put in at the cabin. Perhaps that act of caring played a role in our eventual individual recoveries from drugs, despair, and destructiveness. At the very least, it was a symbol of the communication that continued between us during the five years we were divorced.

For two years Joe lived on practically no money. In order to make his car payments he sold off sections of the land— which I soon purchased from the individuals who'd bought them. He lived at my house on Foulis Street, where I supplied the food. He used credit cards that I paid off. I couldn't just watch him slide away and not take care of him.

We were very distant from one another, though. I felt bitter and jealous, and I drank. He was addicted to Valium. But both of us had kept these drug dependencies secret from one another.

Joe was getting his strength back, however. He'd been without work for two years when he decided to join the Air Force Reserves. He needed the two or three hundred dollars a month he could earn by working one weekend a month. He also knew that flight training would involve drug tests, and that would help him get off Valium.

He was still taking every opportunity to be with other women. Once while on a trip for the Air Force he called me up late at night very drunk, with his female companion giggling in the background. That call hurt my feelings deeply. I was still jealous of his other relationships.

But I also knew that his new occupation was doing him good. At one point the Air Force took him to the wilderness of the Pacific Northwest for survival training, so for a while he got to live out the fantasies of apocalypse that had obsessed him. In these war games he was left alone in the wilderness for days with only a parachute and a pocket knife. When he was "captured" he was put through the rigors of a prisoner-of-war camp. This role-playing of an "end-of-the-world" fantasy seemed to help him regain his self-respect. Seeing these changes in him, I gradually began to let go and turn to myself.

For my part, I was totally absorbed in my work. I felt bitter toward the men who discriminated against me, and justly so. For instance, when I reported an attempt by Rodney to pinch my breasts with a pliers, my supervisor, Barry Semour, told me that if I couldn't handle it I would get transferred. Although he was later demoted by Shell Oil for refusing to act on my sexual harassment report, and as a consequence resigned, at the time his response confirmed my mistrust of men. I became only more determined to excel, however, and I threw myself more vigorously into my work. Although I drank heavily during my weeks off, I slowed down while on the job. Furthermore, I came almost to accept my isolation and as a lease operator was actually spending many work hours in the peaceful swamps alone. I began to see a therapist and to read books about self-empowerment, like those by Edgar Cayce.

Joe's growing independence was clear when he took a full-time job with the Air Force and rented an apartment near the base in a town fifty miles away from me. Although I still struggled with feelings of sadness and jealousy, I was glad he was beginning to enjoy his life again. I helped him move and even donated household goods.

Perhaps what enabled us to grow together again was the acceptance of our separateness. Our anger with one another over the past four years was caused by the inability of each of us to control, or even influence, the other's actions and decisions. That led us to want to hurt one another, to undermine one another's independence. Finally, though, we were each learning to accept the separateness, and out of that, our real need for one another was able to spring up anew.

When Joe's step-nephew, who lived in Pensacola, was in a terrible accident, leaving him a quadraplegic, his parents flew into Pensacola to stay with him. Joe asked me to come stay in his apartment with him, leaving my house for his brother, sister-in-law, and niece to occupy. I willingly agreed to help his family in that crisis, so for the next two months, when I was not at East Bay, I stayed with with Joe in his apartment. This grief gave us the opportunity for a new life that we had been subconsciously searching for.

Our drug dependencies were finally exposed the night he woke up to discover that I wasn't there. I hadn't been able to set up a secret storehouse of liquor in Joe's apartment, as I had in my home on Foulis Street. So, late at night after Joe was asleep, I crept out to go get a drink. When I got back with a number of rum-and-cokes under my belt, he was sitting in the easy chair smoking a cigarette.

"Where were you?" he asked.

I admitted the truth. I'd gone out to get a drink.

"Have you got some kind of problem?" he asked next.

"Yes, I do, Joe."

He was surprised at my story, surprised at the deception that had led him to think everything was normal.

"The liquor bottles in the cabinet at your house weren't emptied quickly," he pointed out.

"No, they weren't, Joe. I kept the bottles I drank from in the laundry room, under my bed, and in the trunk of my car. You didn't know they were there."

"Barbara, I can help you. I don't want an alcoholic for a wife."

That's when he told me that he'd been addicted to Valium for three years without my knowledge and had managed to break the addiction while living at the cabin. I was shocked at the news. I knew about the doctor's prescription of an anti-depressant five years before, but I hadn't realized that he'd continued to take the drug. With horror, I realized that my friends had kept his problem from me because they thought they were protecting him.

Joe did help me dry out. For three days he kept me inside the apartment without a drink. The "cold turkey" detoxification was painful, but I endured it because with honesty sprang new hope. For the first time in years Joe was no longer the enemy but a friend who wanted to help me. My job at Shell became less a bone of contention. As I stayed in his apartment, our mutual support and our enjoyment of one another grew. Within a few weeks we had agreed to live together in the cabin in the forest.

The "Foul-is" house was sold. At the cabin we began a new life. We built pens to raise chickens and ducks, and we even got a new dog. When we were remarried, we made a vow never to hide anything from one another again. The ceremony took place in the same courthouse and by the same Justice of the Peace just one week shy of our original anniversary.

Women realize that success requires determination in the face of constant pressure and are willing to persevere. B.J. was an example of that willingness to succeed through sheer tenacity and exceptional personal effort. She was always ready for new work challenges and took deep personal pride in her accomplishments.

Her high motivation and high personal standards ought to have made B.J. a highly prized employee. Yet she was forced to persist while being overlooked for raises and promotions, thus enduring pressures that would have embittered and soured many other people. Still, in spite of the discriminatory patterns in the workplace that denied her new opportunities to learn and earn, she kept on trying.

In justice, however, the workplace should not place such burdens on any worker's morale and determination. While doing the work required and developing as an employee offer legitimate pressure and challenges, sexual and personal harassment and prejudice are illegitimate pressures.

These illegitimate pressures drain a woman worker's energy, tax her concentration, and burden her spirit. Women's determination to perform well at a job should not be taxed and drained by such social pressures in the workplace unrelated to the job itself. If freed from the pressures of sexual harassment and discrimination, a woman can focus her determination and willingness on being a productive and successful worker.

9

MOVIN' ON UP: WORKING AS A LEASE OPERATOR

✺

By the time B.J. approached the final step in becoming a lease operator, she had managed to gain some respect from many of her co-workers. She had broken a barrier by joining an all-male work force and then by proving that a woman could do the manual and the technical work well. Although changes in society and the law opened the door for her, her successes were based on her individual merit, determination, quick thinking, and hard work.

Unfortunately, many of the challenges she now faced were unrelated to the new tasks of her job. The challenges continued to be in the form of insults to her sex.

✺ I'd been working as a lease operator in the marshy area of Block 24 for about six months when I saw the notice posted on the corkboard: instead of reporting to East Bay at the beginning of my next hitch, I was to go to Morgan City, Louisiana, for seven days of intensive, formal training in lease operation. It was the final step toward my dream of becoming a permanent lease operator. I leaped and yelled in exultation when I read that notice. Before the end of the week's shift I received a voucher for lodgings and meals as well as directions to the Holiday Inn where Shell had reservations for its employees in training.

During my week off I had time to think about the upcoming training and become anxious. Lots of people failed the training program and washed out as lease operators. My mind kept dwelling on that. One senior production operator with twenty years' experience was sent for special training in fluid measurements; he did so poorly in that training program that he left in the middle of the week, trumping up an excuse that bad weather in the Gulf demanded his attention. His supervisors told him when he showed up there that he was going to have to go back and pass the class.

I had no idea what to expect because no one told me what the formal training would cover. Still, I'd studied all the literature available in the East Bay library and knew, at least with the rational part of me, that I had enough knowledge and experience to carry me through. A person's good sense doesn't always overcome his or her fears, though.

I was nervous about driving over to western Louisiana, and although I left Pensacola on Wednesday in plenty of time, I got lost a couple of times in small Louisiana towns and didn't arrive in Morgan City, a boat terminal dominated by Shell Oil needs, until after dark.

The training classes began at 7:00 A.M. and lasted until 5:00

P.M., with breaks and an hour for lunch. Eight of us were lined up along both sides of two long tables with the instructors at the end. We were led through disassembly and reassembly of various parts by means of charts, slides, and films. We each got two three-ring binder notebooks six inches thick, and we were expected to learn all the material before the final exam.

The students in these classes came from all over the United States: Nebraska, Texas, Michigan, California—everywhere. At points where offshore techniques differed from land-based techniques, the group was separated into different sub-groups. Although other students came from offshore facilities, I was the only one from East Bay as well as the only woman.

The instructor pointed to me as an example on the very first day, saying something about the way I'd been brought into the oil production industry, as it were, on a high tide, and that I had found myself a nest. He insinuated that I was hired only to satisfy affirmative action quotas. From that moment I felt ostracized.

Being a "first" at something is always a mixed experience. I *was* outstanding. I had broken a barrier, proving that women as well as men can indeed succeed in oil production. I also knew that I'd broken the barrier through individual merit: determination, intelligence, and hard work. But "outstanding" also means standing out. That certainly became clear during my week of lease operator training at Morgan City. While everyone else formed into a friendly group for lunch and evening study and recreation, I was left by myself.

In the evenings all my colleagues went to dinner together, then sometimes studied or went to bars together. In the mornings as classes were beginning they would laugh and kid around about the events of the night before. The instructor got into the act by passing out aspirin for their hangovers. He always skipped me, just as the men never suggested that I join them. I would eat a solitary Big Mac and fries and return to my room for an evening's study. The men also developed a friendly rivalry about their scores on tests. When tests were returned, they would pass them around to one another so that they could inspect one another's performance. Although I was scoring in the mid- to low nineties, no one ever asked me my score. I just sat there with a smile on my face, but the pangs of loneliness were acute and made the week seem endless.

In this setting I was able to watch that perennial human pattern, people forming a circle based on perceived common interests. The men who studied and conversed together believed they were alike and that I was different. In fact, I had the same interests, knowledge, and goals they had; I could tell the same interesting stories of crises in the oil field, dangerous repairs, and feats of strength and intelligence that they bantered about with one another. I had the same questions, concerns, and anticipation about the new work as they did. Yet they perceived me as different, in spite of our common experiences and values, simply because I am a woman.

And their perception of our difference made them turn away from me rather than toward me.

I puzzle over that phenomenon still. Why do human beings avoid what is different from them and seek out only what is like them? Why must our friends be only the people we have something in common with? Why do we befriend, love, and marry only those we can "identify" with? And in doing so, don't we plant the seed of the relationship's destruction? For that quest for shared or common traits will ultimately uncover traits, preferences, and habits that make us different—if only in subtle ways—from one another. What happens then? Rifts in friendship, break-up, divorce?

Shouldn't people learn to be attracted by other people's differences, not repelled by them? After all, another person's differences from oneself offer a tremendous opportunity for learning. A person of another race, sex, national background, or religious affiliation can call one's most treasured and most unexamined ideas into question. What a wonderful opportunity for growth!

I mulled these ideas over in my isolation while I studied as hard as I could. By the end of the week I'd passed with an average of 93. I proudly took my certificate to the Production Foreman at the beginning of my next hitch. He was just as proud to designate me the first woman Lease Operator B in the Gulf of Mexico.

I had made it, and intense satisfaction flooded me all week long. Yet in the back of my mind a little voice nagged that my promotion to Lease Operator B skipped over the level called Maintenanceman A, a promotion that had been kept from me for years. From that I learned that an injustice lives long beyond its superficial remedy; people ought to beware of perpetrating one. As much as possible, I silenced that voice and enjoyed my double jump in pay and my new authority to work production platforms solo and to train other lease operators.

For the rest of my tenure at East Bay, I worked in the marshy areas of Block 24. I became familiar with the diverse structures and equipment, the snake-like canals, the dense grasses called roso, and the wildlife. The wildlife, most of all, took getting used to. Although waterfowl and raccoons charmed and even befriended me, the huge rodents called nutria rats revolted me. Alligators and snakes shared their habitat grudgingly, and I was always particularly wary of them. But seeing the way some of the Shell workers treated the wildlife there, I began to understand the reptiles' animosity toward humankind.

For instance, I used to ease the solitude of the shifts on Platform I by sharing my tuna fish, fruit, and crackers with a bold raccoon I named "Rocky." I came to think of him as my pet. I could coax him to climb up my pants leg with a Vienna sausage, his favorite treat. Somehow, Rocky put out the word that dinner at B.J.'s restaurant was worth a try, because soon a whole clan of raccoons came with him whenever my boat pulled up.

However, my partner, Rodney, who worked the twelve hours I was off, hated the raccoons. I suspected that he was afraid of them because he insisted, preposterously, that they were of the bear family and would eat people. I agreed that they were scamps—clever thieves who once popped the tops on four cases of soda that had been left on the platform while a work gang repaired a nearby well. But they certainly didn't deserve the fate Rodney forced on them.

Rodney actually turned the platform into an enormous electric chair and executed the harmless creatures! He ran a wire from the platform's power source to the metal grating of the platform. He situated a switch for the current near where the boats were docked. The raccoons would come running when they heard the jo-boat motor, thinking I had arrived. If it were Rodney arriving instead, he would flip the switch, and any raccoon on the grating would die. For a long time after that I had no pets. But there was nothing I could do to protect them or stop him.

I did have my own fears of the fauna that populated those muddy canals and grassy thickets. Snakes and alligators were

threats to my health that I took seriously. During the cooler
months of spring, snakes gravitated to the platforms. They
would emerge from their winter's hiberation very cranky and
in search of warmth. The gas and oil pipes, warmed by the
friction of the liquids flowing through them, were snakes' favorite resting places. I often found them coiled around pipes
on the platforms. I learned to inspect every well jacket or
platform carefully before I began a repair. Once I found a
deadly water moccasin as thick as my arm coiled seven times
around a main pipe that needed my attention. With the snake
determined to hold onto its warm resting place and with such
a grip on it, I had no alternative but to kill it. Such snake
sightings were so common that I carried a snake stick with me
everywhere.

Work in the marshes entailed wading with hip- or chest-
waders through dense grasses and deep mud and water. I would
have to hack my way through the marshgrass with a machete
or scythe. It was exhausting work when also carrying pipes or
equipment, so if I ever encountered a snake, as I often did, I
would kill it rather than taking the long route around it. I was
risking my life daily, after all, in close encounters with the
reptiles of Block 24.

This ever-present danger was very clear the night I singlehandedly repaired a gas leak deep in the swamp.

It was about 1:00 o'clock in the morning. The people in
Block 27, sixteen miles farther out in federal waters, had called
the night supervisor at the island's main office to report that
the pressure in their gas lift lines had in an hour dropped from
its standard level of 1,400 pounds to about 1,000. The gas lift
system ran off the compressors at the island. It fed natural gas
under 1,400 pounds of pressure to all the wells in the East

Bay area. The gas was injected down into oil reservoirs to lift oil up and out. Since the pressure was created at the central facility, and the entire gas lift system ran off it, any drop in pressure anywhere in the maze meant big problems for platforms and wells everywhere. Each platform was equipped with automatic sensors and controls that responded quickly to significant drops in pressure by automatically shutting down the platforms. If this automatic shutdown were to take place throughout the system, at least a full day of production would be lost before the wells could be started up again.

The night supervisor had begun making calls to all the lease operators in the system, collecting data from each site and instructing them to begin checking their areas to locate the leak. My charts showed that I was 250 pounds down from the normal pressure.

I climbed in my boat and began the search for the needle in the haystack. The air was chilly—about 55 or 60 degrees—because it was spring. All the alligators and snakes had been coming out of hibernation. In the last few days I'd encountered many of them, every one in a snappish mood. It was not my favorite time of year for a late-night boat ride.

I methodically travelled the canals of my area, which I had checked just an hour before. The night was moonless, although the stars provided a faint light, but I had a spotlight on the boat. However, I was using my ears, not my eyes, to conduct the search. A gas leak big enough to affect pressure twelve miles out in the oil field would be as noisy as Old Faithful, I knew.

After fifteen or twenty minutes of midnight riding down one canal after another, I heard it—a tremendous roar. I cut back the engine on my boat to an idle and directed my spotlight toward the sound. Sure enough, there was swamp water and mud being blown twenty feet into the air by the tremendous pressure of the natural gas leaking from the line. I quickly called in my location to the night supervisor and then shut off my motor and my radio immediately, because the merest spark from an engine or electrical equipment can ignite any gas in an area. I drifted to the well jacket structure about sixty feet away and began the procedure for closing off the broken gas lift line.

First, I closed all valves leading to and from the well itself. That didn't stop the leak, telling me that the problem was not with the well itself but with the gas lift line running into the well. I had to find one of the block valves that are installed along every pipeline for emergencies such as this. Unfortunately, I had never actually made repairs to this particular line before, so I didn't know exactly where the valve was located. My only option was to trace the line from the well itself.

I jumped down into the dark, cold, muddy water from the eight-foot-high well jacket. In most circumstances, I would have had chest-high waders to keep me dry and safe, but they were in the locker on my platform, and there was no time to go get them. I had to act now. The bottoms of these swampy canals are mucky, so I sank down to my knees in the soft, cold mud. With every step I took, the mud clutched at my shoes.

I located the gas line coming from the well jacket, and with my hands I traced it as it descended into the water and then lower into the mud. I proceeded step-by-step, my hands groping along the line. I was leaning so far over that I could almost kiss the dark surface.

What dark creature would emerge from those inky depths to meet my embrace? I was terrified.

But the work had to be done, and I was the one responsible for doing it.

I groped along the line until I was so close to the leak that mud and water were spraying over me. I then had to circle the geyser and try to pick up the line on the other side of it. I made a guess based on the general direction the line had been taking about where it might be, then dragged my feet through the mud until I hit it. Once again, I bent over and groped along it. The muscles under my skin were contracting with repugnance and fear.

Finally, I found the valve I'd been looking for and closed off the pipeline. The plume of mucky water stopped bounding into the air. But that was only part of the job. I sloshed back to my boat and rode back to my platform. I shut the gas lift lines that came into the platform and substituted another pressure system to keep the platform going. Then I returned to the site of the break with a clamp, to repair the pipe temporarily until the work gang could get to it in the morning. By this time, it was almost 2:30 A.M.

Alligators or not, I once again went into that cold, black water. The clamp I carried was like a length of pipe split along its length, with a lip that allowed it to be bolted together once it had been fitted over a pipe. Since the break in the pipe was under water and mud, I was working blind. My fingers were cold and clumsy in the fifty-five-degree water, but I managed to get the nuts screwed onto the bolts and tightened down with my wrench. When I opened up the valve again to return the gas flow to the line, bubbles boiling to the surface showed that my repair was not perfect. But pressure would build back up in the gas lift system, keeping the oil platforms throughout the oil field in operation.

I was very relieved to have completed my work without ending up as some alligator's midnight snack.

My feeling toward reptiles was not hate, but a healthy respect. In fact, I did respect the ecology of the area, and I wanted to help reduce Shell's damage to that ecology. I knew that if the company thought it could save money by protecting the environment, it would.

Saving money was clearly the motive compelling Shell to cooperate with the Environmental Protection Agency to stop burning excess oil in oil pits made in the marsh. Oil pits about half the size of a football field and surrounded by three-foot-high earthen dikes were located at several spots in Block 24. They were holding areas for any oil drained from a broken pipeline or container. About once a month the oil would be laced with gasoline and diesel oil, then set afire. This was the standard practice for disposing of the oil. Thus the oil was wasted while the atmosphere was polluted with the billows of black smoke. Sometimes, too, the earthen dikes that bordered the pit broke down during heavy rains, allowing the oil that was standing waiting for burning day to leak out into the Gulf. At times crews spent days trying to clean up after such accidents. Not only was the area of the oil pit ruined by this burning practice, but much perfectly good crude oil was wasted, simply because the company hadn't worked out an ecologically-minded procedure for storing oil that had to be drained from lines under repair.

The lease operators in the area were all brought together to discuss alternatives to the practice. An engineer first inspected the sites, and then the company set up a special meeting of the lease operators in Block 24 to develop alternatives. The operators wanted to eliminate the oil pit and restore the area to its natural condition. I was very pleased to be a part of this change, for I objected strongly to the oil-burning, and so I showed up at the meeting ready with suggestions. We brainstormed and figured out a procedure for bleeding lines into a series of vessels of graded pressure levels, thus allowing the oil to be saved and used. While I worked at Platform I, I watched the oil pit gradually returned to a more natural state. Eventually, plant and animal life would replace that ugly scar on the marshland.

Platform I itself underwent dramatic changes, most of them through my initiative. I'd been working as a lease operator in Block 24 for a year when I was assigned to the lease based on Platform I. I felt a sinking feeling when I first heard the news that Jim, the older operator on Platform I, was going to retire. Being the newest certified lease operator B, I knew I was in line for the job. No one wanted to work Platform I because it was the oldest structure on the block, a wooden platform with manually-operated, outdated equipment situated deep in the swamp. The worst sort of accidents could happen there. Pumps rather than pressure gradients controlled the flow of fluid, demanding mechanical skill from the single day and night operators, whose responsibilities at other platforms and at more than a hundred wells in the lease area prevented them from being there all the time. Furthermore, the holding tanks, unlike more modern, enclosed tanks, were open at the top. That meant they could overflow into the water if the pumps failed.

I didn't like it, but I accepted the tough assignment as a challenge. For the next three years I participated in the complete modification of Platform I, and then Platforms P, Q, and O, which were in the area. The engineering department implemented many of my ideas. The pumps and motors that had

179

been used to move the oil through the lines were eliminated and the oil through the platform made to flow by means of pressure gradients, as in most other platforms. No one thought that this principle would work, but it did. New manifolds were built and set into place, and new decks were constructed. I had helped make Platforms I, P, Q, and O safer, better places to work by talking to gang pushers, foremen, and engineers to help them see how the company's economic and safety interests could be served.

I was clearly a lease operator who knew my business. The fears of failing that had plagued me during my training period had evaporated, replaced with a firm confidence in my worth and a pure joy in the work itself. Two years after my promotion to Lease Operator B, I was sent to the next lease operator's training program and again emerged with certificate in hand. My promotion to Senior Production Operator earned me a raise to more than sixteen dollars an hour. With holiday and overtime pay I had an annual income of almost $40,000, the most money I had ever made in my life. I was proud of my work performance and took great pains to instill that same pride in one's work into the people I trained.

My achievements didn't protect me from ongoing harassment and discrimination. It abated somewhat when I became a lease operator trainee associating with the more mature lease operators of Block 27, but it returned full force when I was assigned to work along with men my age and younger in Block 24.

One incident between me and my trainee, Dan, illustrates the kind of harassment I had to put up with. As Senior Lease Operator I was often asked to train lease operators. It was not a favorite job, because having someone trailing me slowed me down. Usually, a trainee had a lot of questions.

Not this one, though. He couldn't have been less curious about the work. I soon found out he had other things on his mind. Dan was a big fellow with a full beard, blond hair, and blue eyes. He'd earned a reputation for telling jokes and playing tricks when he worked with Lowell on Platform A. Today we were headed to Platforms I, P, Q, and O, all in the swamp. From these platforms we might face long trudges in hip or chest waders through alligator and snake territory to check flow lines. I was definitely not in the mood for a prankster's tricks.

Today our job was to change the charts. Each well's output was charted by a Barton recorder, a rotating paper cylinder with a graphic pen that moves as the flow fluctuates. Every week the lease operator ran the jo-boat out to each well to change the paper, read the chart, and make adjustments if the well wasn't producing to maximum capacity. It wasn't a difficult job, but it was technical, and it did require boating out to every well.

I drove "Red," the thirty-five-foot boat that was mine to use, while Dan sat by and listened to my instructions about the operation we were going to do. As I landed the boat at the first well, Dan touched my rear end. My muscles froze, but I told myself that it could have been an accident and climbed out.

But it wasn't an accident. It happened again at the next well, and at the third it became a caress. I flared up, grabbed a twenty-four-inch wrench that was lying nearby, and shook it in his face. "If you don't keep your hands off me, I'll crack your skull. Do you understand me?" This was a problem that no one but me could handle.

Dan withdrew, subdued, but he sulked the rest of the day. I did all the work on the charts while he refused to pay attention and offered no help with the work. I explained the pumps, generators, vessels, and piping that collected gas and oil from the wells and transferred it to Central Facilities for further processing. But he wasn't interested.

"This one is definitely a dud," I thought to myself, but hiring and firing weren't my job.

When we had finished checking the charts and returned to the platform, I went inside the office to start the paperwork and have lunch. Since Dan had left me to take care of the boat myself, he was already at the desk. When I walked in, he pointed to his crotch. "Look."

An erection was bulging in his coveralls.

Irritated, I tried again to get him to shape up. "Listen," I said as firmly as I could, "I don't have time for your foolishness. I have work to do. Now change your attitude or I will take you back to the quarters and the boss can send you somewhere else."

For three more days I dragged Dan around. He continued to sulk, but I wasn't concerned. His attitude was his problem, not mine. I would get the job done and forget him.

And I did. But evidently, while we were working, he was quietly planning a trick to gain revenge.

The next week I was training a much different fellow. Dale was eager, serious about his work, ready to learn. We worked well together and liked one another. On the second day we sat down with the brown paper lunch bags packed that morning by the cooks at Central Facilities, ready to relax for a while. I ripped my bag open, as was my custom. A large, handmade dildo dropped out and clunked heavily on the desk between us. We stared at it in open-mouthed surprise.

The dildo was enormous—at least a foot long, two or three inches in diameter, and as brutal as a billy club. It was an ugly, dark-grey color, fashioned from splashtron barrier material used for repairs on equipment. If someone had been trying to get me angry, it had worked.

"Do you have any idea who did this?" I demanded of Dale.

"No," he answered, shocked. "And it probably won't be easy to find out."

Remembering my brush with Dan the week before, I quickly devised a plan. "Keep this to yourself," I told him. "I have a pretty good idea who did it, but we'll just let him give himself away."

That evening as I docked my jo-boat, Dan came down the walkway with a look of mischief in his eyes. "I heard you got a surprise in your lunch bag," he grinned.

I spat back, "Then you must be the son-of-a-bitch who did it, because neither me nor my trainee told anyone."

Dan laughed mockingly in my face but denied responsibility. "I do know who did it, though."

"Then you tell him that this isn't the first one I've gotten, but this one just may be going to the supervisor."

Later I checked with Cass, the galley worker who packed the lunches. He was in the dark himself. I also showed it to Jenny and Val, who were disgusted by the sight of that iron-grey, circumcised bludgeon. Then I turned it over to Norman, the night supervisor, for safekeeping. I knew it would be useful in the future, but not for what the prankster had intended.

Insults not only to my femaleness but to my professionalism

persisted, even though after four years of work as a lease operator I'd proved my competence and sound judgement again and again. Besides fulfilling my regular duties, I'd been asked to serve as a member of the first safety team, and I was also recruited to serve as the location's First Responder, an individual licensed by the State of Louisiana to offer emergency first aid in any accidents. My paramedic and nursing background made me a logical choice for these positions, but I was expected to do all the work entailed in addition to my regular duties without any extra assistance or reward in higher pay. I was still "giving 150 percent," as the work gang pushers had often said of me.

And yet my supervisors questioned my judgement again and again in ways that made me seethe with resentment. For example, once the Operations Foreman, Barry Semour, told me to check over a high-pressure gas well that had been closed off for several years in order to conserve reservoir pressure. Geologists and engineers were investigating the possibility of returning the well to production. The Operations Foreman wanted me to investigate the site and the condition of the equipment and report back to him.

To find the well I had to leave my boat tied to some small trees along the canal and wade through marshes until I located it, for over the years tides and storms had filled in the access canal with silt and sand, and I had only a map to guide me. When I did find the well, I discovered a rusty ruin. The lines into the well and the surface safety valve were in such bad condition that they would have to be completely replaced. The structure itself would have to be rebuilt, and a dredge barge would have to create a new access canal.

I returned to my supervisor, handed him my completed

paperwork to direct the work gang's activities, and made my report. Totally dismissing my recommendations, the Operations Foreman assigned Rodney, who alternated days and nights with me on Platform I, the very same task I had just completed. I was dumbfounded at the implication that my research and recommendations were not accepted. I felt even more justified in my resentment when Rodney came back with exactly the same information that I'd brought.

Being mistrusted, questioned, and undermined for years by my co-workers and supervisors took its toll on my good nature. In fact, it lowered the flare point of my temper considerably, and after one outburst I got called on the carpet more vigorously than I got congratulated for a job well done.

It all started with a plan I'd made to increase production in one of the platforms I was responsible for. A four-inch line that transferred oil from P and Q platforms to Central Facilities was causing back pressure, thus slowing down flow from the wells that fed into the platforms. I reasoned that installing a six-inch pipe would reduce the back pressure and allow the oil to flow as fast as the wells could produce it, thus improving production. Furthermore, if a six-inch line were to replace the four-inch one, a back-up line would be available if the primary one broke.

I talked this plan over with the gang pusher assigned to help me make repairs. He thought it was an excellent idea and went to the Production Foreman with it. The idea was passed on to the engineering department, found to be a good investment, and approved. When the new six-inch transfer pipe line was installed and the output increased from 4,500 to 6,000 barrels a day, I felt proud.

At our daily shift change meetings, my partner reported to

Barry Semour, my supervisor, that he'd inspected the work and found that it worked well, but that he had reverted the system to its former state. In a flash, I was on my feet.

"You dumb son-of-a-bitch! What have we gone to all of that expense for, just to have you turn it off?"

Barry Semour barked sharply, "Sit down and be quiet, B.J." Then he agreed with my partner that he had done the right thing. I'd heard enough. Barry didn't even understand what work had been done in the area he was supervising. He was clearly more concerned with protecting Rodney's ego than with getting the job done right. I wasn't going to waste my time teaching them how to do their job. I walked out and began my work day.

Later he came to the platform in question to talk over my "misconduct" with me. I walked him through the changes and showed him the actual evidence of flow rate and output. He couldn't deny that my partner had been wrong in shutting down the larger pipeline.

"You shouldn't have talked to him that way," he said, putting the emphasis on my manners rather than my partner's incompetence. Somehow, I was expected to be Miss Charm of East Bay instead of the best damn Senior Production Operator they'd ever had.

❧

B.J.'s good work and promotions failed to earn her the respect of men determined to resent the presence of women at East Bay. She learned the hard way what many women have been forced to recognize: excellent performance in the workplace will not free women from sexual harassment and discrimi-

nation. Even after they reach long-sought employment goals by accruing a fine record of achievements, they may still be sexually harassed and treated prejudicially by co-workers and supervisors.

B.J.'s accomplishements included risking her life to make dangerous nighttime repairs as well as mastering complicated technical systems. Yet her status with co-workers and supervisors did not reflect their recognition of those accomplishments. Years before, as a trainee in the NAVAIDS program, the pervert on the boat had subjected her to sexual harassment. Now even as the supervising trainer, she was still being subjected to another male co-worker's sexual displays and insults while on the boat. Her higher status failed to have a chilling effect on the gender terrorists, who felt themselves innately superior to her.

That unjust prejudice against women of the gender terrorists among her co-workers and supervisors was persistent. It stood like the Berlin Wall—cold, intractable, unreasoning. A woman's accomplishments, in justice, ought to be appraised and valued rationally, without the blindness of bigotry, and they should earn her respect, trust, and relief from sexual harassment and discrimination.

10

THE BEGINNING
OF THE END

꧁

B.J. found herself almost forced into a formal protest when the company implied that it expected her to testify on its behalf in another woman's lawsuit claiming sexual harassment and discrimination. She found herself in the position of revealing what her co-workers and supervisors had been doing to her. But talking openly about the experience she had endured also meant putting herself in physical danger. In part out of fear for her own personal safety, she felt it necessary to resign. Having to choose between her career and the truth, she chose the truth.

꧁ Even with all the shame and humiliation heaped upon me by some of my co-workers at East Bay, I continued to relish the work itself. Like a single, compelling note sounding in the midst of wildly disharmonious music, or like the incantation of a mantra through a particularly disorderly day, the exercise of my mind and body rooted and calmed me as I climbed up ropes onto well jackets, recorded and analyzed readings from gauges, and adjusted flow valves. My understanding of mechanical systems was constantly being tested by new, unexpected conditions. Problems arose that only I could solve. I felt the exhilaration of responsibility, understanding, authority.

From my first work assignment deep in a mudhole on the barrier island of East Bay, I felt that I was a natural. As I took on each new task, I seemed already to know how to do it.

The rupture that began the afternoon of August 21, 1988, was exceptionally painful because I identified so intensely with my work. Yet when I was called in from my lease in Block 24 to talk with Employee Relations assistant supervisor Beth Hess about Jenny Black's allegations of sexual harassment, I was oblivious to the painful separation from my work that would be the outcome. I was going to be asked to choose between a completely fulfilling job and another woman's quest for truth and justice. No wonder I felt ripped apart by the time my interview with Beth and John Town was over.

They had questioned me about the charges of sexual and gender-based harassment that Jenny filed, and I'd corroborated the facts she'd presented. In fact, once the dam cracked, it burst, and I told them a lot more than I ever intended to about the horrors we endured while supervisors like John Town and Employee Relations personnel like Beth Hess turned the other way. The more I talked, the more long-suppressed anger came to the surface.

By the time I was done that afternoon, I was deeply shaken. I felt soiled by the revelation of the disgusting treatment I had endured, even accepted. Some of those dark secrets of shame and humiliation had been extracted like deep-rooted—and decayed—teeth. My stomach muscles felt as if I had done far too many sit-ups, and for the first time I understood how apt was the phrase "spilling your guts."

From the room where I was closed up with Beth Hess and John Town for an eternal three hours, I fled to the dock and to my jo-boat, "Red." I revved up the engine and sped off for Platform I, which waited for me in the midst of the slow, sleepy, and (most important) *pure* swamp. I craved the comfort of that sanctuary. By the time I got there the boat motor's roar and its bucking against the waves had soothed me into a somewhat calmer state of mind, and I began to think.

To think about Jenny. That damned woman! Didn't she have any sense at all? Hadn't she thought about what she was asking of me when she named me as a witness?

She'd put me in a situation, and I was in trouble like never before. The blindness of her! I'd always tried to help her and look out for her. Now she'd implicated me in her allegations, and I was on the line. True, she'd been exploited by men with no conscience, and I hated watching that happen. At the same time, I'd warned her, that naive, foolish girl of nineteen, but she let herself be manipulated more than she needed to have been. And now I was sucked into the situation along with her.

More than that, my life was in danger. This realization brought me to my feet from my chair on the second deck. Nervously, I began to busy myself with simple chores around the platform, but my mind continued to explore this new and terrifying train of thought.

In the past three hours I had named names and cited dates, places, and circumstances that would cost men their high-paying jobs, their pensions, and maybe their marriages. They would certainly be out for revenge. How easily a murder could be made to look like an accident in that desolate, dangerous work location! I remembered the time I'd almost been burned alive, stuck in hip-high waders in the mud banks of the oil pit while the oil pond flared. I'd survived only by wiggling out of the waders and crawling through the muck to safety. The co-worker who'd been watching from the platform, too distant to come to my rescue, embraced me as I got back to the platform and told me he was glad that I'd made it. But not everyone had. I thought about the three men who died in an explosion at a well jacket. I remembered the time I'd found a very decayed body in the grasses of the swamp.

I wasn't just stirring up false dangers. We women all felt that we survived in an atmosphere of threat. April was always particularly afraid when she was the only woman at the quarters during the nights when an X-rated film was being shown over the closed-circuit TV. She would usually call me at Platform I, where I was working nights, and have me pick her up and take her to spend the night at the platform.

These discomforting thoughts of my vulnerability were disturbed by the sound of a boat approaching. As I tried to release the wrench I'd had been using to tighten down a bolt, I discovered that my hand would not come unclenched easily. I massaged it as I walked to the other side of the platform, where I saw the River Chief, the boss's boat, and Dex Pace, Jenny's former abusive lover, at the controls.

Dex seemed extremely nervous as he came up the steps. His head was cocked to the side uncharacteristically, and his voice was choked. "I heard you were called in for questioning today. I just wondered what you told them."

Yes, the man was scared. But somehow, seeing him before me, the man who had used, spurned, and abused my stupid, innocent friend, my dizzying thoughts stilled. I'd been looking down the long tube of a kaleidoscope, the bits of color shifting while the tube rotated wildly. Suddenly, the rotation had halted, and a simple, beautiful pattern emerged. What was right was right. I had to stand up for the truth.

I looked Dex straight in the eye to assure him that I would not be intimidated. "I told them the truth, just like you better have."

"Oh, I told them the truth, the best I could remember. All that was a long time ago."

"Well, I haven't forgotten anything. And if you need your memory refreshed, I have good notes. You know I talked to you about how you were using Jenny," I said, reminding him of my confrontation with him the weekend after he tried to push Jenny out of a pickup truck. "You told me that it was none of my business."

"Well," he said, as his eyes shifted to the empty water of the canal, "I told them enough."

The man was not there to kill me. With relief, I invited him into the dog shack for a cup of coffee. He accepted gratefully, but when I set the cup in front of him, he could hardly drink it. His hands were shaking it out of the cup.

I followed him to the steps of the platform as he boarded the boat to return to the quarters. Distress disordered his usually firm, competent movements with the boat. At the sight of his pain, compassion softened my firm feelings of justice. "Dex, I'm sorry this happened, but you will deserve whatever comes your way."

"I know, and I'm sure sorry, too," and the man shoved off.

I watched his back as the boat drove into the distance, the slope of the shoulders communicating that he was if not a broken at least a deeply shaken man.

I walked through the rest of my work shift much preoccupied. The regular shift-change meeting was abuzz with speculation about what Beth Hess and John Town had been calling people in for. I held myself aloof. I went immediately to the weight room and lifted as much as I had ever lifted before, then jogged vigorously around the island. While I stood in the shower for much longer than I normally did, I knew I had been trying to sweat the trouble and guilt out of my pores, to burn it up with my muscles, to puff it out of my mouth. Now I was trying to wash it off. But it wasn't going away. I began to cry and couldn't stop.

That night as I packed up everything, wrote my letter of resignation, collected the dildo from the night clerk, weeping all the while, I felt the chemistry within me change. For years I had determinedly dismissed any doubts about whether I should stay at East Bay. When my husband accused me of being stupid and self-destructive by exposing myself to the sexual harassment, I refused to listen to him. Now that I was about to leave, his accusations echoed in my mind, and I was flooded with guilt and self-disgust. I'd been so involved with my work that nothing else mattered. I'd accepted all the misconduct and deviant behavior as if it were normal. I was ashamed, humiliated.

Perhaps a child who has been the victim of incest feels this same mixture of shame and pain, of rage and longing.

My sorrowful final departure from East Bay the next morning was interrupted by the emergence of a new feeling, a feeling that would permeate my experiences of the next three years and eventually almost overwhelm these other, deeply personal emotions. It was shock—profound, open-mouthed shock at the hypocrisy human beings are capable of.

As I stepped off the boat onto the terminal where I had innocently parked my car just four days before, I found a clerk from the offices there waiting for me with a note in his hand. I was to call John Town; the one man who could have prevented everything from happening had left his home phone number and wanted me to call. The messenger escorted me to his office where I could use his phone. "I'll keep everyone out, B.J. You won't be disturbed," he said kindly. I want you to know, too, B.J., that I heard what happened and I sure am sorry."

"Thanks," I mumbled, as I dialed the number on the strange black office desk phone.

John's wife answered. He came right away. "I know you are really upset right now. I know how you feel. You are doing the right thing going home right now. We don't expect you to work feeling this way. You go on home and rest up. I'll be in touch with you in a few days."

How dare this man sweet-talk me! For years I'd worked under stressful, dehumanizing conditions that he could have relieved. All supervisors at East Bay were accountable to him as Production Foreman. Every report of sexual harassment, every act of discrimination, every neglected promotion had ultimately been his responsibility. For years he had done nothing, and now he pretended to know how I felt! I was crying again, as I had most of the night. Had it never occurred to him that I could cry, and had?

Still, I felt humiliated that I was breaking down while talking with him, and in reaction, I began to hate him. I had no respect for his position, a position he had abused. "I called you a liar in front of Employee Relations," I told him, "and that's why I have to quit. I know you'll get me for it. You are a liar, too. You said you didn't know about the sexual harassment incidents, but I know you knew. You knew when Padre broke into my room at night with his pants down, begging me to touch him. You knew when Jay tried to rape me. You knew about Dex Pace and Jenny, because you and I talked about it."

"B.J., I won't get you for for calling me a liar. I've been called a liar before. It doesn't bother me."

Now as I think back, I recognize what drove me to that anger, but at the time I held him responsible for the harrassment. Maybe he truly hadn't known. What I knew was that I was hurt, sad, perplexed, and exhausted, and I was going home. John Town told me that he would be in touch.

It was just 8 A.M. when I climbed into my Cougar in the parking lot and began a long, troubled, and final drive home to Pensacola. Joe and I had been living in our cabin on land deep within state forest property. Every backwoods cabin was on the same rural route, so even my mailing address would not lead them to me. I would be safe there.

I was home by noon. Joe and our friend Brad were enjoying a relaxed Sunday conversation in the living room when I pulled up. Both of them got up from their easy chairs in surprise when I came in the front door. If my being home four days early weren't enough cause for alarm, my swollen, red eyes were.

After hearing the basic facts of the situation and assuring himself that I was not injured, Brad said a caring goodbye. Then Joe began to probe for the details. I stretched out on the carpet while I answered his questions and gradually dropped into a fitful sleep.

The sharp sound of the phone at about 2:00 o'clock in the afternoon jerked me back into consciousness, and from that point on the phone rang relentlessly. It was John Town, wanting to urge me to come back to work, or Beth Hess, wanting me to tell her more about what I had gone through, or the head of Personnel at the home office in Houston, or the Eastern Offshore Division Superintendent, all wanting me to listen to their promises that they would make things right. The phone rang day and night for two days. I knew that I was being taped, although no one ever said so, because they spoke so slowly and distinctly. They were also taking notes furiously; I could hear pens scratching in the background. After two days of talking, I realized that I was being worn down. They were giving me no time to think, to appraise my situation, to formulate my thoughts. In other words, I was still being harassed!

Now I had the sense, though, to protect myself immediately. Joe, who had taken the week off so that he could be with me, drove the forty miles into town to get me an answering machine. From now on I would screen the calls. I would decide whom to talk to and when.

And talk I did. Beth Hess called daily, and I spent hours at a time on the phone with her, going over my allegations. I told her that, in my opinion, the men who had harassed me were sick in the head, and that the company owed them psychiatric care. At the very least, the company had the responsibility to teach them how to treat women co-workers. The only individual I felt real vengeance toward was Ervin Floyd, the man who had promised eight and a half years before to do what was necessary to get rid of me. I saw him as the corrupt source of the discrimination against women among the supervisors. On her side, Beth kept asking me questions, kept telling me who had been fired or reprimanded as a consequence of my and Jenny's allegations, and kept trying to persuade me to come back.

Every moment that I wasn't on the phone, I was talking, talking, talking to Joe and sometimes to Jenny. I was in the grips of an obsessive ambivalence. Had I done the right thing by blowing the whistle? For a while, I would be swamped with regrets, bewail the loss of my job, or feel sorry for the wives and children who were suffering as the men's misconduct was exposed and they were fired. Then I would swing over into anger and be just as fiercely determined to get the bastards as I had a few hours before been regretting their punishment.

Joe listened to me for days, offering his perspective, which was forcefully negative towards Shell. He made a banner that read "To Hell with Shell" and hung it on the bedroom wall of the cabin. "You're damn well not going back to work," he would say to me firmly. "You've never been the kind to accept mistreatment before. You ought not be so weak now." In fact, he wanted me to sue Shell. But I just couldn't see the situation through his eyes.

Finally, though, he got sick of the distorted images. "I'm going back to work, Barb," he said, as he set a brand new cassette tape recorder down in front of me. "I want you to use this. That way maybe you'll just listen to yourself."

I took his suggestion, and while he was away at work I used the tape recorder to talk about my experiences with the sexual harassers off-shore. That sent me back to my journals, where I had recorded dates, names, and places. Jenny also jogged my memory with incidents I'd forgotten. With Joe, my tapes, my journals, and Jenny, I was surrounded by mirrors reflecting back at me the true horror of my experience. But still I couldn't see it clearly, and I continued to swing back with nostalgia toward the work itself and with pity toward the poor men's families. I refused to look at the image in those mirrors.

I was ambivalent because I felt guilty for what had happened to me. If a child is the victim of incest, you assume she can't do anything about it. But if the incest continues into her adulthood, it's harder to feel sorry for her. I felt like a fool. I had put up with the harassment. I had been a part of it. My ambivalence was a flight from responsibility.

Time was passing. John Town called me to keep me up to date on who had been reprimanded or fired. He called me one Sunday morning to tell me that he had Dan in his office right at that moment, and that Dan denied ever having caressed my rear end or ever having displayed an erection in front of me.

"How can that son-of-a-bitch deny it? I shook a wrench right in his face and told him that I would give him a concussion if he ever did that again."

"B.J.," said John, "you only worked with him for a week."

Then I realized that he had called in the wrong Dan. He was speaking to a man I had trained just a few hitches before I left, a man who was indeed a consciencious worker.

When John Town finally confronted the "Dan" I had been referring to, Dan admitted his behavior. He also admitted his role in planting the dildo in my lunch bag and named the man who had made it. John told me he fired both of them on the spot.

News like this was both gratifying and terrifying. I knew that I was making enemies. Shell's Employee Relations Manager called: "Please let me come talk things over with you," he asked. "My suitcase is packed, the plane is on the runway, and I can be there in less than an hour." But I was terrified that someone with blood on his mind would find out where I was. I'd insisted that our shotgun stay loaded by the door from the moment I got home that Sunday, and I threatened to empty both barrels into him or anyone from Shell who stepped onto my property. I had to protect myself.

I did offer to see them in the offices of the Human Relations Commission in Pensacola, however. I'd contacted that agency, explained the situation, and told them that Shell was asking to meet with me. The director offered to set up the meeting with Shell's Employee Relations personnel, and to be there herself, along with her agency's lawyer, to monitor the meeting. She wrote Shell a letter explaining the arrangement. They refused. They wanted to see me alone. But I didn't want that, and Joe agreed with my decision.

Beth Hess repeatedly offered me positions at other Shell locations off the Gulf Coast. In fact, the company would have sent me anywhere—Brazil, or North Africa. I missed my job. I wanted to go back.

But the fear of retaliation was always uppermost in my mind. Finally I told her, "If you can guarantee my safety, I'll go back to East Bay."

"We can't guarantee your safety," she said. "But if you don't come back to work, we're going to have to fire you."

The hypocrites were trying to make it out to be my fault!

At that fatal moment, it was as if all those mirrors that reflected my situation back at me—Joe, Jenny, my journals and tapes—had focused sunlight on pine straw, and the tinder finally ignited. My ambivalence resolved. I got mad, once and for all. I understood where responsibility truly lay. They had let this happen to me. I had only one choice: to take them to court.

I left the cabin for the first time in three weeks. I came out of hiding to call on every lawyer in town, looking for one who would agree to sue Shell Oil. They all said they couldn't go to court without a "Right-to-Sue" from the Equal Employment Opportunity Commission. Obviously, the Equal Employment Opportunity Commission was the next step.

I called Jenny Black to find out how far she had proceeded in her own grievance. She'd gone so far as to hire a New Orleans lawyer. However, she had not yet filed an EEOC complaint. We agreed to drive over there from our homes in Florida to file our complaints.

During the three-hour drive we talked and talked, charging one another up for the inevitably ugly, prolonged battle. Jenny's anger was more profound than mine. Her favorite revenge fantasy was to get Roy Barker up on the witness stand, where she could accuse him and shake her finger at him, as he had shaken his finger threateningly at her so many times before.

As I imagined the courtroom and the questioning, I became uneasy. How could I possibly tell people about the man who had come into my room at night and stood over me with his penis hanging down, begging me to touch him? How could I talk about the man who took his penis out of his pants every time we were alone? But in New Orleans, my legs moved me so fast from the parking lot to the EEOC office that Jenny couldn't keep up. Something in me was determined to get myself there before I backed out.

At EEOC we learned that we could file complaints only

about events that had happened in the last six months. I hadn't realized that such a brief statute of limitations on discrimination and sexual harassment existed. So many horrors that I wasn't going to get to use as evidence! I was desolated.

Our case worker then explained that if our charges on events of the past six months were found upon investigation to be true, we could then file additional charges about events that had happened before those more recent ones, even back to the first day we were hired. So we would have to wait until the initial investigation was completed before we submitted more information.

From the EEOC office in New Orleans, Jenny took me to the office of her lawyer. It was, ironically enough, in a building across the street from One Shell Square. The lawyer was a short, plump, freckled, strawberry blond in her early forties with a five-star record in sexual discrimination suits. She thought we had a strong case. She said that the journals and audiotapes I had kept for years made the very best evidence in court. Her outrage at our experiences and evident commitment to fighting sexual discrimination won me over too quickly, and I let her get by with shabby business practices.

She explained that some law firms will accept a client's case on a contingency basis. That means that if the suit is successful, the law firm gets a certain percentage of what the client wins in court. However, her law firm was too small to take our suit on those terms. She asked instead for $5,000 up front and $75.00 an hour. She promised a written contract and monthly statements, neither of which she provided. However, I agreed to her terms. I'd decided that I would spend every penny I had to get my day in court. I contributed $3,000 and helped persuade Jenny's father to loan her the other $2,000, and we began our quest for an EEOC letter of "Right-to-Sue," which might take six months.

I soon discovered that quitting a job, filing an EEOC grievance, and initiating a lawsuit can consume all a person's time. I spent the next four months writing letters to protest one problem or another with Shell Oil, with the EEOC office in New Orleans, with my lawyer. First, although Shell Oil had kept me on the payroll during the weeks the bosses were trying to persuade me to come back to work, they fired me when they found out that I had filed a grievance with EEOC. When they sent me my final paycheck, the bank refused to cash it because the numerals and the written amount didn't correspond. I wrote a letter of complaint and sent it back. They sent a second check. Same problem. Again I wrote a letter and sent it back. I saw what they were doing. They were hoping that I was hard up for money and that I would give in to them out of financial distress. Fortunately, I had some cash in reserve.

Their squeeze play included blocking my unemployment benefits. The Louisiana State Board of Unemployment refused me my unemployment checks, saying that the company had denied my right to them. In my communications with Employee Relations, though, I'd been told that Shell would not refuse me unemployment benefits. I sent the Unemployment Board copies of letters Shell had written to that effect, but still the Unemployment Board refused me unemployment compensation. After lots of calls and letters, I finally got fed up. "Fine!" I said. "If Shell won't let me get unemployment benefits, I'll sue them for that, too." This threat evidently hit the mark as my complaints had not, for soon after that the checks began to come.

With Shell and the Louisiana Unemployment Bureau both harassing me, I expected at least some support to come from EEOC, but in fact the exact opposite was true. Every letter I got from EEOC about my grievance began with the words, "This is to inform you that the commission is considering dismissal of your charge" and gave me only three days to respond. My anxiety on reading these letters was intense. I didn't understand the process or the reason for the threat of dismissal. I responded to each letter frantically. I was beginning to feel steamrolled by these unresponsive government agencies and corporations.

I reached out for help, placing calls to national offices of the National Organization for Women, the American Civil Liberties Union, even the National Association for the Advancement of Colored People. No one really had any specific advice.

By December my initial charges against Shell had been found valid by the EEOC and yet agency representatives still had not written a letter of "Right-to-Sue." They were holding it back even though their investigation was complete, because regulations allowed them up to six months to grant such a letter. They were using the time to pressure me into going back to work at Shell, saying that I was refusing what should be an acceptable compromise. Shell had promised to rehire me with no prejudice and to give me a $40,000 payment for pain and suffering. Shell had also promised to remedy the discrimination by firing, demoting, or reprimanding guilty parties. Why was EEOC advocating for Shell? Did Shell have

203

the EEOC office in Louisiana in its pocket? I began to wonder.

At any rate, I refused Shell's offer for my own good reasons. First, I simply didn't believe that Shell would follow through on its promises, since it had operated with no conscience for eight-and-a-half years. Second, I felt that Shell ought to be held accountable for ignoring the reports of sexual harassment and the ensuing problems for the past eight years. And finally, Shell Oil would not guarantee my safety. I had a right to sue.

From the very beginning, I wanted my day in court. I wanted the opportunity to accuse all those who had intimidated me, pinched me, threatened me, forced themselves on me, or colluded in the harassers' actions. I wanted to tell my story before judge and jury. A financial settlement was absolutely irrelevant. I was willing to pay off my lawyer's fee week by week if necessary. Justice seemed the only salve for my troubled soul.

After four months of frustration at EEOC's refusal to grant a right to sue, I wrote my United States Congressman. His office could initiate investigations of federal agencies, and it did so immediately. The EEOC in Florida began to investigate the EEOC in Louisiana, and, as if by magic, my "Right-to-Sue" letter appeared in early April of 1989. Now my lawyer could file charges. It was Holcombe and Black *vs* Shell Oil Offshore, Inc. and Roy Barker.

A date for the hearing, a "docket date," was set, to my chagrin, for May of 1990, an entire year away. Still, in eagerness, I jumped into action. I made seemingly endless statements, called "interrogatories," and had them notarized, I reproduced some of my journals for evidence, and I gave my lawyer lists of witnesses. I was ready to tell my story.

Meanwhile, I had found another blue-collar job in the vicinity of my home so I could pay my lawyer's bills. She occasionally contacted me to tell me of Shell's most recent offer. Each time, the company offered me more money. Each time, I told them that money wasn't the point. My lawyer didn't like that at all. "You'll get more money if you settle out of court than you will if we go to court." When I persisted in my quest for a day in court, she seemed to lose enthusiasm for my case. She was also persuading Jenny to accept Shell's offer of money, telling her that since her case was weak, she would never have enough money to pay the legal fees.

The lawyer also wasn't seeking out the witnesses I had told her about, wasn't researching the case. I was doing all the work and dragging her along like a dead weight. She wasn't going to be prepared for the court date in early May 1990.

In fact, the court date came and went without my ever being notified of it. I discovered that in a civil case, the defendent can cancel the first date by claiming insufficient time to prepare a defense. Clearly, Shell was stalling, because the company had been investigating my claims since I had walked off the job a year and a half before.

I came down hard on my lawyer. Jenny accepted Shell's paltry settlement—something that really unsettled me. My lawyer let me down, too. I demanded that we immediately begin preparation for the next docket date. At my insistence, she and a professional photographer visited the East Bay facility to make photographic records of locations where many incidents had occurred. She also arranged to take depositions, official statements made in front of lawyers and a court reporter, from John Town and Roy Barker. She would question them in the presence of Timothy Hightower, Shell's highest legal defense from Houston. I would be questioned the next day by

Shell's lawyer in her presence. So by pressing her I was able to start the chain of events that brought my ordeal to an end.

We gathered on the morning of May 16, 1990, in the conference room of my lawyer's office. It was on the third floor of an old New Orleans building. Large windows overlooked Shell's corporate offices. A fantasy of popping a rifle off in that direction flashed unbidden through my mind as I took my seat in a plush chair around a large glass-topped table. Quickly, I focused my attention instead on the thirsty house plant sitting by the window. Since I'd been allowed to observe the deposition only by permission of Shell's legal counsel, I knew that I had to keep control of my temper.

My lawyer, Shell's lawyer, and Roy Barker, the first Shell employee scheduled to give his deposition, took their seats. I was in blue jeans and a shirt. Timothy Hightower looked the way a lawyer ought to, with a small mustache and a dapper three-piece suit. A young court reporter by the name of Mary swore Roy Barker in and then took her seat at the recorder. Throughout the hearing she looked straight ahead and for the next two days never flinched or reacted, in spite of the ugly stories and crude language she heard. Had I been in her place I would have giggled or smirked or something. Her lack of reaction struck me as strange.

The process was the same as in a courtroom. If my lawyer asked a question that the Shell lawyer didn't like, he would object to it. Both Roy Barker and John Town were questioned that day. Shell's lawyer instructed them before they began to tell the truth. I knew that Shell had coached Jenny when she was called as a witness in a case between Shell and another oil company. At that time Shell lawyers told her that if she was asked any questions that would turn against the company, she should say that she didn't remember. I also recalled that when John Town and Beth Hess approached me about Jenny Black's allegations, they told me that I owed my loyalty to the company.

But to my surprise, they didn't lie. At one point that day, my lawyer took me into her office and told me, "I'm going to have a field day with these people. They're telling the truth. I didn't expect them to tell the truth."

The second day brought my turn to make a deposition, and I followed suit by telling the truth as well. I'd been poring over my journals late into the evening, nervous that I would make a mistake. I took the journals along with me in an attache case, which also held other documents and evidence, including the dildo.

After about an hour of questioning, the Shell attorney asked me about all the notes in my attache: "Do you have complete written records of the eight years and nine months of working offshore, B.J.?"

"You bet I do. You have some copies of what I have."

He turned to the court reporter and told her that he would ask no more questions. The rest of the conversation would be off the record.

As he questioned me, he had been leafing through a notebook four inches thick. "I know where you got all of those pages, Tim," I told him as the court reporter packed up her materials. "You got them from Beth Hess. She was taking notes while I was talking to her on the telephone. But I'll tell you one thing that isn't in that book."

"What's that?" he asked.

"The fact that I tried to settle all this with her three years ago, but she wouldn't have anything to do with me." I was

207

referring to her evasion of me, of Val and Jenny, when she visited East Bay.

"Is that the truth?" he said.

My lawyer spoke up. "Yes, that's in the interrogatory statements submitted earlier."

"I'll have to go back and check that out," Shell's lawyer said.

"You tell me where Beth Hess is at today."

He said, "She was promoted and sent to Houston."

"So crime does pay, doesn't it? How can you represent these people? You know they're dirty. You know the job you're doing is dirty." I was getting worked up.

"That's just it," he answered. "It's my job."

"I had to give my job up. If you think they're wrong, you should give your job up, too. What would you do if someone had done these things to your mother or your sister? How would you feel?" I was close to tears by this time.

Tears seemed to be shining in his eyes, too. "I'd kill 'em," he said, sincerely.

I came to think that Shell's lawyer was on my side. But not for long.

Because after another hour of his questions and my answers, he paused pensively for a minute. I was still absorbed in the memories of the incident we'd just been talking about, so it took a few moments for his announcement to sink into my consciousness.

"Mrs. Holcombe, Shell Oil Offshore will not appear in court against you."

I sat dumbfounded for an instant, but then, with a flash, red the color of flames flooded my vision. Without knowing what I was doing, I was on my feet lunging at him. I was in a frenzy. I'd waited for two years for my day in court, and now he was snatching it out of my hands.

My lawyer and Joe, who'd been allowed to enter as the court reporter left, were on their feet, too. They had to drag me out of the conference room to get me under control. I was weeping wildly.

Gradually, I calmed down, and we were able to return. Tim moved away from the windows, where he'd been staring at the edifice of One Shell Square. Between sobs, I listened to him lay out the facts of the matter again. "You can't kill them, B.J. If you push to go to court, we just won't show up. It all comes down to money."

"I don't want your goddamned money," I said bitterly. I jerked my thumb toward Joe, who'd been inconspicuous in the back of the room: "Talk to my husband. He does."

Tim Hightower's eyes rose to the man he hadn't even noticed before.

"Howdy, Bud," Joe nodded, his eyes narrowing, and Tim Hightower's face collapsed.

After the conference broke up, my lawyer couldn't contain her excitement: "We're going to be rich, B.J." I felt so wrung out, exhausted, and defeated. How could she be so elated? She and I had very different values, I realized. While I wanted justice, she was in it for the money.

Her next communication to me proved it. In an overnight mailing she sent me the contract she'd promised from Day One but had never provided. This contract described our arrangement as being a contingency basis rather than the per-hour basis she originally arranged. Now that she knew how big the pie was going to be, she wanted a large slice.

In negotiating the settlement, Shell demanded that I not

reveal the terms or the amount of the settlement for ten years or face a penalty. I've never gotten a chance to make my experiences public before judge and jury. The day I signed on the dotted line was a dark day for me.

Although the women I worked with at East Bay are no longer there, some women still work as offshore production workers for Shell Oil, and they call me often for advice or to act as a confidante. For the most part, the changes made at East Bay are small. The men do not touch the women or expose themselves in front of the women now. Portable toilets are available on platforms in order to comply with Coast Guard pollution regulations. This privacy benefits everyone, especially the women. But no woman has every been promoted above lease operator. Shell claims that no woman has ever become qualified for promotion, that I was their only chance.

I think about my career often. I hear from my friends offshore that Nick Claire, hired just six months before me, is now being trained as an Operations Foreman. This man who discriminated against me will soon be a chief supervisor in the area. If I hadn't left, perhaps I could have been promoted and then used my position to counteract the effects of bigots in the supervisory staff.

B.J.'s search for justice clearly took her through strange waters. But any search can bring a woman to the brink of a dirty pool. Sometimes, her only alternative is to dive in, resigning herself to trailing along some muck when she

emerges. That was certainly the case for B.J. She had her heart set on a "day in court" because it represented justice. She wanted to expose publicly the inhumanity of gender terrorism as she had experienced it.

Ironically, B.J.'s case was so strong and her evidence so substantial that she had no alternative but to settle her case out of court. Shell Oil simply wouldn't allow its own callous indifference to its female workers to be exposed as B.J. could expose it.

For B.J., in one sense not getting her "day in court" felt like a defeat, because she wanted the opportunity to let people know how some men behave when a woman penetrates an all-male work force. But she discovered another hard reality of the search for justice: the journey is not over when the dragon has been confronted. B.J. had to find her way home to herself again.

CONCLUSION:
THE CONTINUING SEARCH
FOR JUSTICE

☙

The long, difficult healing from the trauma of vicious sexual harassment and discrimination can take years. But that healing is hastened by speaking out. No longer burdened with a secret shame or resentment, no longer holding it inside, more and more women who have been held hostage by gender terrorists have washed away the residue of unpleasant emotions. Opening the doors to our fear and shame in order to expose sexual harassment and discrimination becomes women's only course of action.

Shame and fear must give way not just to anger—although anger is a stage in the path—but to a personal commitment to make things right. Every woman who faces gender terrorism can and must find the personal courage to search for justice for her own sake and others'.

Gender terrorism can be exposed only by the women who have experienced it. They must expose gender terrorists because in doing so they can protect themselves and other women from the same kind of discrimination they have endured.

If women can accept the social problem of sexual harassment and discrimination as an opportunity to participate in the search for justice for all women, each one will grow personally from the effort. By accepting the injustice that has entered her life as a personal challenge and by dedicating herself to meeting the injustice in a self-affirming way, she will give herself an opportunity for new learning, new self-esteem, and a new relation to her co-workers, friends, and family.

Even more basic, in working to transcend the gender terrorism in her life a woman will come to understand her own womanhood more completely. Since the perpetrator of sexual harassment and employment discrimination has targeted her femaleness as the problem, a woman who accepts this challenge naturally gains a fuller idea of her own selfhood as a woman. As she gradually transcends the situation the gender terrorist has defined, she will also gradually clarify her beliefs about her womanhood and her individuality as a person— her sense of strengths, her limitations, her ideals, and her rights.

Only by putting their experiences of sexual harassment and discrimination on the record do women make their viewpoint part of their company's and their society's history. Their silence, on the other hand, protects people who have committed an injustice and allows them greater freedom to commit more injustices.

By being willing to reveal their experiences of sexual harassment and discrimination, women make small changes possible. By speaking out, women can help all of us identify the patterns in workplace behavior that make up gender terrorism. Women who speak out in a search for justice also help to identify the techniques used against women in the workplace and to develop strategies to free us all. And a woman who files reports, grievances, and even lawsuits can benefit indirectly from learning how her institution's or company's power structure works. Although she may discover that the organization or institution she is working within is not ready to consider seriously the social injustices taking place within its ranks, her efforts may lay the groundwork for some other woman who finds herself in the same position later. Especially after hearing in October, 1991, the allegations by Law Professor Anita Hill about Supreme Court nominee Clarence Thomas's sexual harassment of her, women are beginning to realize that confrontation is necessary. Women who have been held hostage by gender terrorists know from Anita Hill's example that the search for justice leads through a dark forest, but that in pursuing her quest, each one of us can illuminate the path for those who follow behind.

APPENDIX:
WHAT TO DO IF YOU SUSPECT THAT YOU ARE A VICTIM OF SEXUAL HARASSMENT OR DISCRIMINATION

by Charmaine Wellington

1. **Distinguish legitimate from illegitimate work requirements and interactions.**

   A student visits a professor's office for help on a project and ends up getting pinned against the wall. Another finds a friendly, receptive individual who invites her to return, praises her performance, and encourages personal confidences of a more and more intimate nature. The first case is very easily identified as sexual harassment, but the other is far more murky. Seduction is often difficult to distinguish from support. A masher can wear the mask of a mentor.

   And initially-professional relationships can evolve into unprofessional ones. An administrative assistant's role can gradually include more personal tasks—scheduling parties, arranging for dry cleaning, and, finally, accompanying the boss to public events.

In all these cases the women students and secretary accepted the perpetrator's behavior. The first student complained to her friends but not to anyone in authority. The second student persuaded herself that her professor's advances were merely friendly until he suggested sex. The third followed her living companion's amazing recommendation to go out with her boss. In all these discriminatory situations the women hesitated to name them for what they were and to act appropriately.

The more we want the job, the more likely we are to find excuses for the behavior of bosses and co-workers who make us feel uncomfortable. This is true of anybody. One of the authors of this book admits that she endured her supervisor's overbearing, long-winded criticisms of her performance, always administered behind closed doors, because she convinced herself that it was part of her training. The other author weathered insults from the first day of employment because she considered her ability to "take it" a sign of strength. We both know now that you don't need to take it.

Stay alert to your feelings. One sign that you are experiencing harassment or discrimination is the amount of time you spend dwelling on your relationship with your boss, co-worker, or professor. Are you thinking a lot about the reason the perpetrator might be behaving in ways that make you uncomfortable? Are you making excuses: "He's going through a divorce," or "I know that his blood pressure has been troubling him"?

If you are feeling uncomfortable, admit it to yourself,

and stop trying to understand *why* it might be happening. It doesn't matter why. Regardless of our training to be compassionate in our relationships, the work relationship is different. In a workplace, mutual respect is as important as understanding. If a boss is making demands upon you that you are uncomfortable with, he is failing to offer you respect. Your compassion will not change that as effectively as will your respectful confrontation of him about the behavior. Besides, by asking him to work with you respectfully, you may help him identify his own personal problems and thus remedy them. Passively accepting his outrageous behavior may not be as helpful as confronting it.

2. **Keep records of incidents.**
Fair-minded, responsible people may respond well to such conversations, but perpetrators of discrimination and harassment may not. By making your boss, co-worker, or professor aware that you have problems with his behavior, you may discover that his attitude toward you has changed. He may begin to control himself, or he may escalate his harassment. The wisest course is to expect the worst and prepare for it.

The most self-caring action you can take is to keep a work diary. Make a daily record of whatever affects your work performance and every incident that occurs between you and the perpetrator. Make it detailed. Record dates, times, and locations of events. Write down exactly what happened, even including dialogue, if you can. Also write down the work you were assigned, the length of time it took you to complete it, and the way your supervisor or professor responded when you turned it over.

As much as possible, follow up face-to-face meetings or phone conversations with memos summarizing what happened and the conclusion you have drawn from them. Keep copies of these memos, and also keep copies of anything the perpetrator writes in response.

Written records work like magical keys to open doors that would otherwise be shut in your face. Supervisors, personnel departments, lawyers, and representatives of state and federal offices listen better when you have paper to back up your testimony. Documents—even memos you have written yourself—carry as much punch as eyewitnesses, who may be difficult to come by. B.J.'s lawsuit was victorious when Shell Oil's lawyer saw that her highly detailed, horrifying testimony was backed up with thick bound journals and other records. My own claim of discrimination convinced a conservative Republican administration's Office of Civil Rights only because I had a letter from my supervisor in which he had documented his venomous attitude toward me. Like Anita Hill's testimony in Clarence Thomas's Supreme Court appointment hearings, your word may not be enough. Put it in writing.

3. Define your objectives.

The point of any quest is to get where you want to go. But where is that? Do you want to hold your job but get the gender terrorist to change his behavior? Do you want to find a different position in the same company? Do you want to ensure that he never does to another woman what he has been doing to you?

Your goal may not be easy to figure out at first, though, since harassment or discrimination may have come unexpectedly into your life. And your goal may change as the situation itself changes. But figuring out what you want is a helpful step because clear goals may guide your reaction to the gender terrorist's surprise attacks.

Soon after B.J. took her job, she realized that she wanted other women to be hired to work with her at East Bay and that she wanted to achieve the position of Lease Operator, a key responsibility in the offshore oil field and a position that had never been held by a woman. I realized soon after joining the university that I did not wish to become a tenured member of that particular department but that I did want to recover the good reputation that the gender terrorist had deprived me of. Both B.J. and I realized our goals before leaving our positions. That left us with a sense of accomplishment, even as we both grieved the loss of our careers.

Of course, objectives may shift as a situation of discrimination or harassment evolves, but defining them serves an important purpose: in the presence of a belittling, undermining, or manipulative supervisor or co-worker, a clear sense of purpose helps ground your identity. You know what you want, and you know that you will get it.

4. Communicate expectations and request changes.

Besides figuring out where you want to go, you need to figure out how to get there. That usually means that you need to know how you want the situation to change.

How should your professor behave when you are in his office, for instance? Would you like him to stop touching you while he talks about your paper? If so, make that request. Has your boss taken to telling dirty jokes to you?

Tell him simply that you don't like it and you want it to stop. Do you want your supervisor to step in when your co-worker refuses to cooperate with a woman? Ask for his support. Identify what needs to happen to make your situation more comfortable, and then ask for it. Do it in person—and then in writing. If the gender terrorist is very hostile or irrational, then write a letter or memo only. Whether you talk to him before writing, or simply write, in either case be calm and specific. Say simply what he is doing that is objectionable and how you want it to change. Don't discuss motives or feelings; his divorce, or whatever, is no excuse for his unfair treatment of you.

Difficult as it may seem to face the gender terrorist, you may need to take this step whether you think it will do any good or not, because it lays groundwork for the future. If you were to file a grievance through a union, personnel office, or student affairs office, for example, the hearing officers would want to know if you had talked to the gender terrorist yourself. The point of this step and the next one is to give the company or the department the chance to solve the problem itself. Most outside agencies, such as the courts or the Equal Opportunity Commission, will not step in unless you have already tried to get the company itself to help you and it has refused or failed to do so.

5. **Research the organization's policies and procedures.**
The bigger the organization you work for, take classes from, or apply to, the more protected you are. Since the early 1980s most large companies have been developing policies against discrimination in hiring, promotion, and treatment of women workers. Visit the personnel office and ask for

the company's policy statement on discrimination and sexual harassment. If your company is unionized, your union steward will be the person to ask. Ask for information about filing a grievance, too, if you feel comfortable doing that. Even if you do not plan to file a grievance, it helps to know something about the process and the paperwork. After all, your goals might change in the future.

If you work for a small business owned by the perpetrator of the discrimination or sexual harassment, your city or county seat may have a Human Relations Board (the name may vary) that may offer advice and information. A lawyer or consultant at a Legal Aid office could also give you advice about steps you might take in the future.

Don't be reluctant to do this research just because you think lawsuits and the like are ugly. Remember that you are just gathering information. Having a form and filing it are two separate steps. You need information about all your choices in order to make a good decision about how to proceed.

6. **Use the formal and informal power structures to protect yourself.**
Formal structures: If you are being harassed by a boss or a co-worker, find out who his boss is. Whom does he report to? Who evaluates his work? Even the head of the company is sometimes accountable to someone else—partners, a board of directors, shareholders who meet regularly, or even the company's lawyers. Remember that if some worker is harassing or discriminating against you, he is putting that company in jeopardy. Other people may want to know.

The gender terrorist's superior may be a person who can

help you. If the perpetrator persists after you have asked him to stop, you might consider making a report to his superior. Don't count on being kindly received, though. In many cases, that individual will stand behind his subordinate and blame you, as the whole nation saw was the case when Anita Hill presented her complaint during the Clarence Thomas hearings. This step, however, like your previous one, is necessary. You have to give the company a chance to protect you before asking an outside agent to help.

Informal structures: Important as policies and laws are, the best they can do is prevent a perpetrator from behaving illegally. They really can't change the atmosphere of a workplace by making people feel differently about one another. That takes peer pressure. In some cases you may be able to find support in a person with influence in a group. Try to identify the friends of the gender terrorist; is there anyone among them whom you also trust? Could you let that person know indirectly that you are having a problem with his friend? Be subtle and indirect, if you can, for this person may feel the need to defend his friend against direct, angry accusations.

A second course of action would be to identify the person in the group who seems to be respected or well-liked. Decide whether that person is likely to be sympathetic to your situation and, again, let that person know what is happening. The key here is to identify the individuals who have some social influence over the gender terrorist.

I think it's important not to keep the experience secret, although B.J. disagrees. At least, confide in some co-workers or fellow students, particularly any women who also work for or take classes from the gender terrorist. In my experience, this "gossip" can uncover a pattern of harassment or discrimination, as it did once in the restaurant where I was working to put myself through college. One slow evening, as several of us sat at the waitresses' table, I mentioned that the restaurant owner had called me back into his office a few days before and then grabbed and kissed me. Every other waitress at the table exclaimed that he had done the same thing to her. Evidently, he was testing to find out who would kiss back. Shocked at this information, the head waitress stormed furiously to the back office to confront her boss. Often the gender terrorist who is pinning you against his office wall every time you are alone with him is taking the same advantage of other women, and, like you, they have been keeping it to themselves. Don't protect this behavior with your silence.

7. **Make reports and file grievances.**
A grievance or a report is an official complaint. It is reviewed by officials. Now, officials may not care whether the gender terrorist has been vicious, petty, aggressive, violent, or downright inhuman. All they will care about is: has he broken any rules, policies or laws? When you file a report or a grievance, don't expect that anyone will share your pain and outrage; get that sympathy from your friends. Instead, expect officials only to do their jobs fairly, and keep at it if they do not. If you have been keeping a diary and writing memos, and if you have copy of the company's policies on harassment or discrimination, you will be well-prepared, and filing a grievance will be far less troublesome. You will already have a clear record of everything that has

taken place, complete with dates and places. (Reading it over may strengthen your resolve, too.) A grievance or some other official action usually requires a complete description of the problem. Consider a day-by-day summary of events as one possible way to organize your statement.

With each event you recount, refer if you can to company policies or regulations that have been violated. Your union representative or even a friend with a lot of common sense could go over your statement with you. Friends may get impatient with your complaints about your situation, but they often love to help you take action. As with any written document, present it well. If possible, have someone double-check it for spelling, grammar, and other aspects of good writing, and have it typed.

8. Find witnesses.

A grievance or a lawsuit often stands on two foundations: whether a law or policy was clearly violated and whether you have factual evidence in the form of documents— memo, tapes, and so on—and corroborating testimony. Gender-based discrimination grievances rest more heavily on the first: your rights must be clearly violated, and often you will have to prove that those violations took place specifically because you are female. It's not easy.

Sexual harassment grievances rest more heavily on the second, evidence. This is often difficult to present, because rarely does a gender terrorist perform before an audience. But if you complained to a co-worker immediately after an event took place, or if someone overheard him make cruel remarks to you, you may be able to convince that person to include a statement along with your grievance.

Many people will refuse to do so, though, fearing for their jobs, just as you may. Don't blame them. Your co-worker may not be the hero you are.

Re-entering the world of normality after an intense trans-formative experience may not be easy. Not all the changes that have taken place in you will be accepted by your friends and loved ones. Your social relationships may have changed as a consequence of the personal and social conflicts you may have undergone. On the other hand, you may know more clearly on whom you can rely. And one ally who has proven herself through the whole process is yourself.

PUBLISHER'S NOTE

This logo represents Stillpoint's commitment to publishing
books a _____ e
system _____
to live _____
ingful _____
all lif